BERLIOZ
his life and times

BERLIOZ
his life and times

Robert Clarson-Leach

MIDAS BOOKS
HIPPOCRENE BOOKS
New York

In the same illustrated series

BACH	Tim Dowley
BARTOK	Hamish Milne
BEETHOVEN	Ateş Orga
CHOPIN	Ateş Orga
DVORAK	Neil Butterworth
ELGAR	Simon Mundy
HAYDN	Neil Butterworth
MAHLER	Edward Seckerson
MENDELSSOHN	Mozelle Moshansky
MOZART	Peggy Woodford
OFFENBACH	Peter Gammond
PAGANINI	John Sugden
RACHMANINOFF	Robert Walker
RAVEL	Burnett James
ROSSINI	Nicholas Till
SHOSTAKOVICH	Eric Roseberry
SCHUBERT	Peggy Woodford
SCHUMANN	Tim Dowley
TCHAIKOVSKY	Wilson Strutte
VERDI	Peter Southwell-Sander

© Robert Clarson-Leach 1983

First published UK in 1983 by
MIDAS BOOKS
12 Dene Way, Speldhurst
Tunbridge Wells, Kent TN3 0NX

ISBN 0 85936 149 7 (UK)

First published USA in 1983 by
HIPPOCRENE BOOKS INC
171 Madison Avenue
New York, NY 10016

ISBN 0 88254 666 X (USA)

Printed and bound by
The Pitman Press, Bath

To my musician wife, Daphne,
in appreciation of her great patience

Contents

Acknowledgements

The author and publishers wish to thank the following for help in the research for this book and, where applicable, for granting permission to quote copyright material and reproduce illustrations.

Madame J. Bran-Ricci who allowed the author to photograph Berlioz's guitar at the Musée Instrumental Conservatoire National Superieur de Musique, Paris; Marie Françoise Egret of the Conservatoire National Superieur d'Art Dramatique for permission to photograph the reconstructed concert hall; Anne-Marie Couturier, Hachette, Paris; the Controller of the Comédie Française Theatre; Miss Catherine Haill, Theatre Museum, Victoria and Albert Museum, London; Bernard Brandon, Horniman Museum, London; the Library of the British Museum; Victor Gollancz Ltd and Alfred A. Knopf Inc. for permission to quote extensively from Berlioz's *Memoirs*, translated and edited by David Cairns; Messrs J. M. Dent & Sons Ltd; Oxford University Press; Messrs Thames & Hudson Ltd; BBC Publications; Hachette (Section droits de reproduction), Paris; the Public Record Office; Novello & Co., Music Publishers, London; Burnett James for his work on the text.

Acknowledgement of sources for illustrative material is gladly made as follows: Delta Productions page 44; Hachette 14, 16, 20, 33, 37, 39, 46, 48, 76, 77 (below), 80, 81, 84; Colette Masson 41, 72, 110-11; Public Record Office 74; SPADEM 19; Victoria & Albert Museum 95, 96, 97, 99, 100. The extract from *The Ballet of the Shades* (Berlioz/edited Hugh MacDonald) on page 109 is reproduced from the vocal score by permission of Novello and Co. Ltd. Unless otherwise stated all photographs and illustrations have been supplied by the author and are his copyright material.

1 Childhood

An ancient inhabitant of La Côte Saint-André was quoted in the issue of the *Nouvelliste* for 2 September 1934 as offering the following observation:

M. Berlioz? Ah yes . . . my grandfather often spoke of him. They used to say in the town that the Doctor's son had gone to the bad, given himself up to music, playhouses, Paris, and Lord knows what else. It was rumoured that his mother never got over it. He'd come back once in a while. There was a lot of whispering when he passed by: no one dared speak to him any more . . . he looked out of humour with the place. But he didn't do too badly after all, did he?

It was not surprising. Berlioz was one of the first of the great European Romantics, almost a prototype. And such figures were frequently regarded, especially by simple folk, with some awe, often outright trepidation. In more senses than one they were 'suspect', yet looked up to as a mixture of the semi-divine and wholly profane, both in their characters and in their works. It was a familiar situation that has not been entirely quashed even today. And in any case, Berlioz himself was, as a leading Romantic, very well aware of his own position.

It was in the small French provincial town of La Côte Saint-André in the Dauphiné, between Vienne, Grenoble and Lyons, that Louis Hector Berlioz was born, on 11 December 1803. His birthplace stood on the side of a hill with mountains to the south and the ice-capped peaks of the Alps to the north.

The infant Berlioz was propelled into an unstable world. In May of that year England, under the rule of George III, had renewed the war with France. The French Revolution had broken out in 1789, leaving the French people with a strong sense of rebellion, epitomized by the storming of the Bastille on 14 July. By 1790 the power of the established Church in France had been broken. Both in Britain and in France men were now able to declare an interest in anti-religious philosophies without automatically being thrown into prison for blasphemy. The Church had to battle on open ground with those who advocated atheism. Politicians tended to side with the Church in denouncing 'free thinking'. Shelley, who had been sent down from Oxford University for issuing a pamphlet on 'the necessity for atheism' was obliged to settle in Italy, Jean-Jacques

A view of the dramatic landscape typical of the Dauphiné district of France where Hector Berlioz was born.

Rousseau, for similar though not identical reasons, went to Holland. Church and Government alike in England and in France shared a fear of radical thinking.

This schism, atheism confronting religion, was reflected in the Berlioz family. The father, Louis Berlioz, a much respected and highly skilled surgeon, was an openly declared atheist, but the mother, Marie-Antoinette-Josephine (*née* Marmion) remained a staunch Catholic who extracted a promise from her husband that he would not deliberately try to wean their son from the Faith. So for the first seven years of his life the boy was brought up as a strict Catholic. The fact that he eventually left the Church and abandoned the Faith seems to disprove, at least on one level, the Jesuit theory that the years of childhood are indelibly formative and that what the child is taught will be imprinted for life.

Throughout his adult life Berlioz claimed to be a calm agnostic and, except in a purely professional capacity, kept himself at a safe distance from the Church. Compositions in later life, such as the short Christmas oratorio *L'Enfance du Christ*, are usually regarded less as a direct expression of religious faith than as a backward glance at the unquestioning beliefs of his childhood. (*L'Enfance* is in fact reputed to have begun as a four-part piece sketched for organ, first scribbled down at a party. Only later was Berlioz struck by the primitive mysticism and decided to add words.)

By the standards of the nineteenth century, the Berlioz family was of average size. Hector had three younger sisters—Margaret-Anne-Louise, known as 'Nanci', who was born three years after himself, in 1806, Louise-Julie-Virginie (born 1807) and Adèle-Eugénie (born 1814), plus two brothers neither of whom survived into adulthood—Louis Jules, born in 1816 and died three years later, and Prosper, born in 1820, who died at the age of eighteen while at boarding school in Paris. Thus Hector was the only male Berlioz to achieve true adult status; even the middle sister, Louise-Julie-Virginie, only managed to live for some eight years, though the other two did reach their middle forties. It was not in fact much below par for families in the early nineteenth century.

As a child Hector attended Mass every day and received Holy Communion on Sundays. He took his first Communion on the same day as his sister, Nanci, at the Ursuline convent where she was a boarder. He was called to the altar first, extremely conscious that he was surrounded by young girls dressed in white. When he had received the sacrament he became aware of the beauty of the music that followed, which turned out to be 'Quand le bien-amié reviendra' ('When my sweetheart returns to me'), a somewhat curious choice for Holy Mass. However, this appears to have been the boy Berlioz's first conscious musical experience, though it was to be another ten years before he learned what the tune was and could put a name to it.

Meanwhile, the outside world went on its more or less demented way. On 14 May 1804 two events took place that were to determine the history of Europe for the next decade and lead to results that would influence it for at least a generation. On that day William Pitt became Prime Minister of England, and Napoleon proclaimed himself Emperor of France (thus greatly displeasing Beethoven, among others). The new confrontation of Pitt and Napoleon made any possibility of peace even more remote. It may well have been fortunate for history that Pitt died in 1806 and that England was much preoccupied during those years with such matters as the abolition of slavery, which came about formally in 1807, and the process of industrialization, for the alternative might have been the annihilation of Europe. Napoleon's dreams of domination led him into the lethal snows of Russia in 1812, and to final defeat at Waterloo three years later. Ten years before that defeat Napoleon's fleet had been crushed by Nelson at Trafalgar in one of the most decisive naval battles of all time. Yet the sea, like all theatres of life, was witnessing rapid changes: steamships were being developed, as steam trains were on land. By 1820 there were thirty-four steamships successfully in operation, a number that increased rapidly during Berlioz's lifetime.

The early part of the second decade of the nineteenth century saw similarly radical changes in the musical world. The death of Joseph Haydn in 1809 marked the end of a musical epoch. Haydn is often referred to as the father of the modern symphony orchestra, the scope and resources of which Berlioz himself was soon to extend beyond contemporary imagination. In any case, a new generation was emerging. The year of Haydn's death saw the birth of Felix Mendelssohn, who Berlioz was later to meet in Italy and Germany, and the following year both Chopin and Schumann were born. Only three years later, in 1813, two of the giants of nineteenth-century music, Verdi and Wagner, saw light of day, the first in northern Italy, the second, who was subsequently to be seen as the main rival to Berlioz in the matter of large-scale music drama, in Leipzig.

At the same time, the British, though much preoccupied by the war with America as well as by the Napoleonic argument, still found time for music, even though the lack of native talent of real stature tended to set them apart from their European contemporaries. All the same, the Royal Philharmonic Society was founded in 1813 and its first official concert given on 8 March. This was an event of some importance, and helped to make England increasingly attractive to foreign musicians. Berlioz himself was in his own turn to be a welcome visitor to London.

That was still in the future. When he was ten the young Hector was sent to the local secondary school, but his father, who had won a medical competition in 1810 with a *Treatise on Chronic Diseases, Cupping and Acupuncture*, was by no means satisfied with the teaching there. He accordingly removed his son and decided to instruct him at home, laying particular stress on languages, literature, history, geography, and some music. From these lessons Berlioz developed a love of distant lands and a romantic curiosity about the outside world. He also showed an ever deepening appreciation of literature in general and Virgil in particular. Louis Berlioz successfully communicated to his son his own love of the Classics, and it was to have a lasting influence on the boy's subsequent development.

The next significant year was 1815: it marked the defeat and banishment to St Helena of Napoleon Bonaparte, and the awakening to the mysteries of music and love in the youthful Berlioz. As he

Estelle Fournier, *née* Duboeuf, with whom Berlioz fell in love when he was only twelve.

14

Berlioz's guitar, now housed in the Musée Instrumental of the Conservatoire de Musique in Paris.

himself wrote in his *Memoirs*, 'Love and Music were revealed to me at the age of twelve'.

The first love of Berlioz's romantic life was Estelle Duboeuf. She was eighteen, six years his senior; but it was love at first sight for the ardent boy. 'I was conscious of an electric shock. I loved her.' Although condescending adults laughed at the unconcealed devotion in Hector's eyes, and his mother teased him unmercifully, he was not deterred.

Estelle's maternal grandmother*, Madame Gautier, owned a small white villa with an old ruined tower in the hills behind. In the summer Estelle and her sister would stay there. Estelle was the younger of the two: she was tall with large eyes, and wore pink half boots that Berlioz never forgot. It all came about because his maternal grandfather, a member of the large Marmion family, also lived at Meylan, so Hector was able to spend holidays there amidst the enchanting scenery, with his mother and sisters and his military uncle Felix Marmion. Above all, he had regular opportunities to gaze at his beloved Estelle. Felix Marmion had not only been a distinguished officer in Napoleon's army; he was also a keen amateur violinist and singer. In later life he and Berlioz became very close.

Berlioz's formal music education began in May 1817. His first teacher was M. Imbert, who had been a second violinist at the Théâtre des Celestins in Lyons. He had moved to La Côte Saint-André and was able to give young Hector lessons in singing and flute

*There is some confusion about the actual relationship. Berlioz suggests that Estelle was Madame Gautier's niece. On the other hand, the Glossary of the Gollancz edition of the *Memoirs* states unequivocally (p.543) that 'It was her maternal grandmother, Madame Gautier, who owned the house at Meylan.' This must be taken as definitive.

twice a day. Imbert's son, a horn player, became a friend of Berlioz; but unhappily he hanged himself and Imbert returned to Lyons in July 1819. His place as teacher was taken by Monsieur Dorant, an Alsatian from Colmar. All his life Berlioz was grateful to M. Dorant, and many years later referred to him with respect and gratitude as 'my old guitar teacher whom I haven't seen for (twenty) years.' The reference to the guitar is notable, as apart from the timpani the guitar was the only non-wind instrument Berlioz ever came near to mastering.

He was now sufficiently well versed in music to understand the complexities of a full score when he saw one. He was also excited by reading the lives of the great composers, including Haydn and Gluck. He was approaching fourteen and his father was becoming increasingly alarmed at his son's active interest in music and his less than enthusiastic regard for medical studies. Louis Berlioz was not the first father to bribe an offspring to change course. If Hector would study medicine seriously, then he should have a new flute. Possibly as an act of musical discouragement, he was not allowed to have piano lessons, and in fact he never became a good keyboard player. His youthful knowledge of harmony and chord progressions was gained from the guitar, while his sense of melody and phrasing came from singing and playing the flute. As a singer he had become an excellent sight-reader, an accomplishment that was to help him find work when he was penniless in Paris.

Louis Berlioz's vetoing of piano lessons did not turn out quite as hoped or expected. Hector was infinitely grateful that he was not just another keyboard manipulator.

My father would not let me take up the piano; otherwise I should no doubt have turned into a formidable pianist in company with 40,000 others . . . and thus saved me from the tyranny of keyboard habits, so dangerous to thought, and from the lure of conventional sonorities, to which all composers are prone.

M. Dorant could play most instruments, with particular facility on clarinet, cello, violin and guitar. Under his guidance, during 1819 Hector became expert on the guitar and could play flageolet, flute and drum with reasonable fluency. He was also beginning to compose, but he was far from satisfied with his work. 'Almost all my melodies were in the minor . . . my compositions bore the stamp of a profound melancholy!'

1819 and 1820 were musically formative years for Berlioz. All the same, in the following year his father finally got him into medical college. He began full-time medical studies in the French capital in October 1821, in company with his cousin Alphonse Robert who, despite being a fine violinist, went on to become a distinguished doctor and did not follow Hector into the precarious world of music.

A contemporary sketch of Berlioz playing the guitar.

For his part, at a safe distance of time Berlioz recorded his aversion to the profession of medicine, his revulsion at the 'charnel house' of the dissecting room, and his lack of sympathy with his teacher of anatomy, Professor Amussat, all in somewhat hilarious terms.

But now it was 1822. He was in Paris. The conflict between medical obligations and musical inclinations had begun.

2 From Medicine to Music 1822-1829

Berlioz settled at 104 rue Saint-Jacques, Paris, in November 1821. Rue St Jacques is on the Left Bank and runs southwards from Île de la Cité, past the present Sorbonne University, the Jardin du Luxembourg, and on to the eastern end of the modern Boulevard du Montparnasse. The rue de l'Ecole de Médecine is at the northern end of rue St Jacques, and in Berlioz's time these narrow streets, so near to the Seine, were liable to flooding. Students often made their way to the river bank to 'eat their sandwiches' and meditate.

The New Year 1822 found young Berlioz at the crossroads between following a medical career and wandering into the exciting world of music. An evening at the opera should have been an innocuous event for a medical student, but for Berlioz a visit to Salieri's *The Danaids* was enough to dispel all medical studies from his thoughts and fill his head with the tunes he had heard. The next day at college he hummed the themes from the opera, and was much too excited to concentrate on Professor Amussat's dissertations on anatomy. Hector's aesthetic feelings, warmed by the music of the opera, shuddered in cold revulsion at the experiments in the dissecting room. He viewed with horror the dead, swollen, purple bodies which were so readily available in the back streets of the slum areas of Paris. He had no stomach for using the knife and the saw in the medical room to dismember those awful human bodies. The opera opened his eyes to another side of Parisian life.

The following week he again went to the opera, this time to hear Méhul's *Stratonice*. But what was really significant was a visit to the ballet *Nina, ou La Folle par amour* by Louis de Persuis; it contained the hymn tune 'Quand le bien-aimé reviendra' that had been sung at the Ursuline convent at his confirmation. The ballet was taken from the opera of the same name by Nicholas Dalayrac (originally d'Alayrac but changed in the interests of circumspection during the Revolution), and the recognition brought back vividly to Berlioz the moment when 'Love and Music were revealed' to him at the age of twelve. And when he discovered soon afterwards that the music library of the Conservatoire was open to the public, his resolve to study medicine was further weakened. 1822 found him studying and copying the scores of Gluck until he knew them by heart. 'An ecstasy possessed me,' he wrote. His father was less ecstatic; on reading his son's letters home about the excitement music held for him, the

The flooding of Paris streets was a sight familiar to Berlioz, though this particular inundation occurred in 1900.

doctor optimistically replied that it would soon pass and that a resumption of medical studies would not be long delayed.

Any real hope of this, however, was dashed when Berlioz heard Gluck's *Iphigénie en Tauride*, written in 1779 and on its first production an even greater success than the 1774 triumph of *Iphigénie en Aulide*. It was by now inevitable that Berlioz would set his own hand seriously to composition, which he accordingly did with a piece he called *Le Cheval Arabe*.

It was a decisive move. By historical coincidence that same year, 1822, saw the birth of a Frenchman who was destined to make as big a mark on the medical field that Berlioz had decided to abandon as Berlioz himself was to make on the world of music. On 27 December 1822, at Dôle in the Jura, Louis Pasteur was born, the son of a former sergeant-major in Napoleon's armies. (Ironically, a twentieth-century opinion poll showed that the French people believed Pasteur to be 'the greatest man France had ever produced'; the once omnipotent Napoleon was placed only fifth!)

In the autumn of 1822 the medical school closed for three months, and Berlioz was never to return as a student. Instead, late in the year, he became a music pupil of Jean-François Lesueur, one of Napoleon's favourite composers and professor of composition at the Conservatoire since 1818. Lesueur was not only to exert great

19

The *grande amphithéâtre* of the Ecole de Médecine de Paris, where Berlioz studied before abandoning medicine for a musical career.

Jean-François Leseuer, professor of composition at the Conservatoire, with whom Berlioz began studying music in 1822.

musical influence on Berlioz but also showed him much personal kindness (in 1828 he paid the fee for Berlioz for the Prix de Rome). It was Hyacinthe Gerono, a close friend and fellow admirer of Gluck, who introduced Berlioz to Lesueur, having first given him some revision in elementary harmony. In that same year Perne, the Director of the Conservatoire, died and was succeeded by Cherubini, with whom Berlioz was to have many a quarrel.

In his *Memoirs*, Berlioz makes fun of Cherubini's speech and attitudes; and there appears to have been good cause, certainly to an arch-romantic like young Hector Berlioz. When he took over at the Conservatoire, Cherubini instituted a regime of sheer puritanism. In his view there was far too much talking between the sexes. One of his directives concerned the library. He recoiled at the idea of male and female students meeting there unsupervised by a teacher, so he issued an order that male students must use the door in the rue du Faubourg Poissonière, and women the door in the rue Bergére.

It led to trouble at once. Berlioz, unaware of these curious new moral restrictions, entered one morning by the door he invariably used—and it happened to be the 'female' entrance. He was in the middle of the courtyard leading to the library when a porter named Hottin stopped him and demanded that he go all the way round the building and enter by the 'male' door. Hector brushed past the man and went into the library. He forgot all about the incident until about fifteen minutes later, when Cherubini himself entered accompanied by Hottin, who identified Berlioz as the transgressor. It is at this point in the *Memoirs* that Berlioz first resorts to his amusing habit of ridiculing Cherubini's broken French.

'Eh! Eh! So it is you! It is you who come een by the door that I weel not 'ave you use?—What—what—what ees your name!'

Berlioz dug his toes in; he refused to divulge:

'My name will perhaps be familiar to you one day, but you will not have it now.'

Cherubini looked as though he was on the point of collapsing in an apoplectic fit as he and the porter chased the young music student round the library tables.

'S-s-seize 'eem', Cherubini cried to the porter. 'I'll 'ave 'eem in preeson!'

That was Berlioz's first encounter with Cherubini. It need not be taken as absolute gospel—Berlioz's imagination was as active in his

Cherubini's tomb in the Père Lachaise cemetery in Paris. Cherubini was Director of the Conservatoire when Berlioz was a student there.

writings as in his compositions.* But there is no doubt that the substance is right; and he certainly did have various altercations with the Director. He may have been prompted to make play with Cherubini's speech weakness in French because he himself was having trouble persuading Parisians to pronounce his own name correctly. They would call him 'Berli-oh', with the 'z' silent. But the name was German in origin and the 'z' was not mute—the proper pronunciation was therefore 'Berli-ohz'. The French had some difficulty with it at first, but as in much else got it right in the end.

Berlioz listened to as much music as he could during the last weeks of 1822. Among the works he heard at that time was Reicha's opera *Sappho*, which he went to on 16 December, significant because Reicha was to become his tutor in counterpoint a few years later. But for the moment Lesueur had charge of his musical training, and his song *Amitié, reprends ton empire* was his first composition to bear the inscription 'Pupil of Lesueur'. It was completed early in 1823.

In the spring of 1823 he visited his parents at La Côte Saint-André. It was an uneasy homecoming; his father was still not certain that his son had finally abandoned medicine and his mother persisted in hoping that Hector would be strong enough to fight the 'evils' of music, theatre, and the moral dangers of life in Paris. On the other hand, the return to La Côte Saint-André revived all his old passion for Estelle Dubeuf, who was holidaying again in nearby Meylan. On his return to Paris, he set to work composing a piece for his beloved, his 'Stella Montis', and by the late summer had completed *Estelle et Nemorin*, in an orchestral version. In the following winter his thoughts returned to the Middle East (his first composition had been *Le Cheval Arabê*) and he wrote the oratorio *Le Passage de la Mer Rouge* ('Crossing the Red Sea'). But he was still not satisfied that he had done justice to Estelle, so he asked Hyacinthe Gerono to write a dramatization of Florian's *Estelle* which he could turn into an opera. He decided to call it 'Meylan Memories', but the finished book and score turned out, in his own words, 'absurd' and the opera never materialized. 'Luckily no one ever heard a note of this composition,' he wrote in his *Memoirs*, and his first published work was the song, *Le Dépit de la Bergère*.

Young and impetuous as he was, Berlioz gradually began to lose his admiration for Lesueur, who insisted on laying down the principles of harmony, counterpoint and composition as though they were universal laws which could not be questioned. Teacher and pupil did, however, share an admiration for Gluck, Virgil and Napoleon. Indeed, a quotation from Virgil could have summed up

*It is generally conceded that Berlioz's imagination frequently took the upper hand in his writing, with the result that his own accounts of his life, especially in the *Memoirs*, are not necessarily accurate and reliable in detail, though they invariably are in essence.

22

The church of Saint-Roch. The choirmaster there commissioned a Missa Solemnis from Berlioz.

the driving forces in the mind of Hector Berlioz: 'Love conquers all, and we too succumb to love.'

Towards the end of 1823, M. Masson, choirmaster at Saint-Roch, asked Berlioz for a Missa Solemnis, but it was not actually commissioned until the spring of 1824. In the first few months of that year he completed a cantata, *Beverley* (or *The Gambler*) for bass voice and orchestra, which he described as 'a very sombre and vigorous piece of work taken from Saurin's play'.

The summer months of 1824 were again spent at home. On his return to Paris Berlioz completed the Missa Solemnis, which was ready by the end of the year. The parts were written out by choirboys, but Berlioz discovered to his horror how unreliable such an exercise could be. Mistakes abounded, so he wrote out the whole

A plaque outside 92 Avenue Denfert-Rocherau, Chateaubriand's Paris home for twelve years.

of it himself; but despite this prodigious labour he was still badly let down by singers and orchestral players and the rehearsal, on 27 December, was a total fiasco. Instead of the 'hundred hand-picked musicians and even larger choir', the promised 'huge forces' turned out to be a chorus of twenty and a handful of instrumentalists whom Berlioz referred to as 'a rabble of musicians'. Henri Valentino, conductor of the Opéra from 1824 to 1831 and the Chapel Royal from 1824 to 1830, had been engaged as conductor. Fortunately, this eminent musician appreciated the potential of the young composer, and promised to help him when he had rewritten the Mass and gathered together a full choir and competent orchestra.

Berlioz wrote furiously to complete the work, only to discover that he had in the end created something too big to manage. Where could he find the singers and players? There was no help from Lesueur, who felt that if he assisted one pupil in this way all the others would expect the same treatment. Berlioz could see no way of launching his Mass, until he had the idea of approaching the vicomte François-René Chateaubriand, a writer he much admired,* for a loan of twelve hundred francs to finance a performance. A copy of Chateaubriand's reply is given in the *Memoirs*:

Paris, 31 December 1824

You ask me, sir, for twelve hundred francs. I have not got them. If I had, they would be yours . . . I sympathize with your difficulties. I love art and honour artists. But talent sometimes owes its eventual success to the trials it has to endure, and then the hour of triumph is compensation for all that one has suffered. Please accept my regrets—they are very real.

Chateaubriand

Berlioz's grandoise ideas were already landing him in trouble. The failure of the Mass was naturally seized upon by his parents, who used it to ridicule his passion for music and as a lever to persuade him to return to his medical studies. His father went so far as to threaten that if he persisted in following a musical career his liberal allowance of one hundred and twenty francs a month would be stopped.

The young man could hardly claim to have lived in poverty on such an allowance. In 1823, bread cost 43 centimes and a packet of salt 25 centimes. In 1827 he shared lodgings in the rue de la Harpe with Antoine Charbonnel, where they lived on 30 francs a month. At that time Berlioz was earning 50 francs a month at the Théâtre des Nouveautés. We can further evaluate Berlioz's allowance by comparing figures mentioned in his *Memoirs* for 16 July 1848.

Paris buries her dead. Even the *Spirit of Liberty* on top of the Bastille has a bullet through her body. The Assembly has just voted a sum large enough to

*The first version of the programme of the *Symphonie fantastique* began: 'An artist . . . suffering from that state of soul which Chateaubriand has so admirably depicted in his *René* . . .'

enable the theatres to reopen and to afford a little relief to the most hard-hit artists. A first violin at the Opéra was lucky if he earned *nine hundred francs a year* [my italics]. He lived by giving lessons.

Berlioz himself received one thousand four hundred and forty francs a year! In 1856, his election to the French Institute brought with it an allowance of one thousand five hundred francs a year—'and that is quite a lot for me!' he conceded.

His musical tastes remained passionately loyal to Gluck and Spontini; he had scant respect for the popular Rossini. He hated the mutilated versions of operas that contemporary Paris loved so dearly. An example of this that particularly enraged him was the hacked and plundered version of Weber's *Der Freischütz* which, under the title

The rue de la Harpe, where Berlioz shared lodgings with Antoine Charbonnel.

Robin des bois, ran for over one hundred performances and made more than a hundred thousand francs profit. Carl Maria von Weber was in Paris during 1824, and Berlioz was much distressed to find that he kept 'just missing' the composer who was to become the 'liberator of Berlioz's imagination' and take the young composer beyond 'the limits of Gluck and his school'. How infuriating it was for Berlioz to discover that whereas the *Robin des bois* version was published in full score, that of *Der Freischütz* remained unpublished.

In the spring of 1825 he had a stroke of luck. A fellow student at the Conservatoire, Augustin de Pons, lent him the twelve hundred francs he needed to finance the Missa Solemnis. De Pons, who came from an aristocratic family, had witnessed the disastrous rehearsal of the Mass at Saint-Roch the previous December. He was impulsive and generous by nature and became as enthusiastic as Berlioz himself for the Mass to achieve the success both believed it deserved. The conductor Valentino, orchestra, choir and singers were engaged, and on 10 July 1825 the Mass was given at Saint-Roch and the youthful composer at last had the satisfaction of hearing his music realized and successfully presented.

After this gratifying outcome, Berlioz next set to work on an opera, to be called *Les francs juges*. A new friend, Humbert Ferrand, wrote an epic poem for him to set and he began 'with unparalleled enthusiasm'. The theme of the project was a study of the secret courts that terrorized late medieval Germany. Berlioz and Ferrand agreed on many aspects of politics, but disagreed on religion, Humbert Ferrand being a devout Catholic. These two collaborated on one other dramatic work, *La révolution grecque*, in the following December. The affairs of Greece were very much on their minds.

It was a time of high hopes and ripening promise. Unhappily only in the case of Berlioz were they to be fulfilled, since these two friends who helped him so willingly at the start of his career eventually died in distressing circumstances. Augustin de Pons married a singer 'believed to be Mlle Saint-Ange' and followed her from concert to concert until she left him for another man. De Pons returned to Paris, the money owed to him having been paid by Berlioz's father; but times were hard and he could only make a meagre living by teaching singing. The Revolution of 1847 took away all his pupils, and in 1848 he poisoned himself. Humbert Ferrand's last years were also clouded by poverty and he became paralysed. He and his wife adopted a child, Blanc Gounet, who as a young man murdered the woman who had mothered him and ran off with her jewels. Ferrand himself died in 1868, a few months after the brutal murder of his wife, and Gounet* was arrested and guillotined.

*A certain Gounet, a friend of Berlioz, lent him 300 francs when he married Harriet Smithson. It is possible that Gounet the benefactor was also Gounet the murderer, but the author has found no firm evidence to prove this.

The time Berlioz had spent on the Missa Solemnis and its production difficulties had distracted him from his studies, and in July he failed the preliminary examination for the French Institute. The Institute was set up under the Revolution (in 1795) and consisted of five academies, of which Fine Arts was one. Berlioz was to campaign four times before he was successful in 1856, although in his *Memoirs* he claimed he made only two attempts. Even when he was finally elected he was a little contemptuous of the whole business. He was pleased with the money, but hardly with the Institute itself: 'Victor Hugo had to knock five times, de Vigny four. Balzac never got in, and Delacroix is still not in after six successive attempts. And the fools who are admitted!'

Hearing about Hector's failure, his father tackled him about it during a holiday at home in the autumn. Dr Berlioz was angry not only with his son but also with his son's teacher. Lesueur, knowing that his pupil was under threat of having his allowance stopped, wrote to the father pleading for both the allowance and the music studies to continue. Unfortunately, Lesueur used religious arguments to support his plea, not realizing that the good doctor was a declared atheist. He received a chilly answer in reply, which began, 'Sir—I am an unbeliever—'.

Things began to look decidedly bleak for the young Berlioz. However, in an extraordinary volte-face Dr Berlioz called his son to his study one November morning and informed the astonished young man that he would be permitted to continue with his musical studies, on condition that if he failed he would choose another career, not necessarily medicine. Dr Berlioz made it clear that he had no time for second-rate poets, or second-rate artists of any kind. Despite his joy at this turn of events, young Berlioz did allow the thought to pass through his mind that his father might be forgetting the danger of producing second-rate doctors. Nevertheless, he embraced his father and readily agreed to the bargain.

Dr Berlioz then disclosed that his wife was not a party to this arrangement. The doctor suggested that in order to avoid a scene, his son should leave secretly for Paris. But Hector's change of mood from deep despair to bounding happiness aroused the suspicion of his sister Nanci. She badgered him until he eventually told her about the secret offer. Nanci could no more keep a secret than her brother, and soon the entire household knew, with the result that his mother absolutely forbade him to return to Paris, declaring—'I shall not have this sin laid to my charge'. Hector could do nothing to change his mother's attitude, try as he might. In a scene he was never to forget his once affectionate mother raged at him:

'Very well, go! Drag yourself through the gutters of Paris, besmirch our name, kill your father and me with shame and sorrow. I shall not set foot in this house again until you have left. You are my son no longer. I curse you!'

Previously Lesueur and young Berlioz had laughed over the motto of the female members of the Berlioz family: 'Respectability comes before everything!' But now it was different, and what he was to describe as 'a moment of horror' made him understand that abandonment of 'respectability' was no laughing matter in 1825. At that time the Church invariably refused permission for actors and actresses to be given religious rites or to be buried in the graveyards of parish churches. Thus Hector's determination to engulf himself in the 'fast' life of Paris and the arts struck deep.

Mme Berlioz took refuge in the family country house at Le Chuzeau, near La Côte Saint-André. Despite an emotional appeal by Berlioz, his father and his sisters, she refused to see him. 'My sisters and I were in tears. It was hopeless. I had to go away without embracing my mother, without a word or a look from her, and with all the weight of her curse upon me.'

In December 1825 he completed *La révolution grecque* ('Scène héroïque'), but he was finding it difficult to live on his father's allowance. He took some pupils at one franc a lesson in solfege, flute and guitar, and by rigidly economizing managed to save enough to pay back six hundred francs of the twelve hundred he owed de Pons. His address had been still at the rue Saint-Jacques, but he now moved to cheaper lodgings in a fifth floor room in Île de la Cité at the corner of the rue de Harlay and the Quai des Orfèvres. He further economized by living on bread, raisins, prunes or dates, which he frequently ate in the open or on the banks of the Seine.

Although the Revolution was more than a quarter of a century old, people were still starving in the streets of Paris. Berlioz could not close his eyes to the situation. He considered the King to be an imbecile and Polignac the puppet master. He was still excited by the reckless vision of Napoleon, with his sense of glory and dream of the

The Quai des Orfèvres bordering the Ile de la Cité.

unification of Europe under France. Berlioz's background and social and family environment made him highly susceptible to the Napoleonic legend. His surgeon–instructor at medical school, Jean-Zuléma Amussat, had served under Napoleon and was decorated for bravery. His uncle Felix Marmion was also an old campaigner with Napoleon in Prussia, Poland, Spain and at Waterloo. These and other veterans fed young Berlioz with tales of Napoleonic grandeur. His music teacher Lesueur refused Charles X's award of the Légion d'honneur because he preferred to keep the chevalier's cross presented to him by Napoleon.

With the literary predilections acquired from his father it was natural that Hector should turn to the poets and writers of the day, especially those in whose works he found thoughts and impressions compatible with his own. He was inspired, for example, by the imagery in the poems of Thomas Moore, which he had recently discovered in translation. Was he perhaps especially impressed with lines such as these?

> The Minstrel Boy to the war is gone
> In the ranks of death you'll find him.
> His father's sword he has girded on,
> And his wild harp slung behind him.

> The Minstrel fell!—but the foeman's chain
> Could not bring his proud soul under;
> The harp he loved ne'er spoke again,
> For he tore its chords asunder;
> And said, 'No chains shall sully thee,
> Thou soul of love and bravery!
> Thy songs were made for the pure and free:
> They shall never sound in slavery!

Or was he still saddened by his mother's curse and the happy days of homelife slipping farther and farther into the past as the present marched on?

> Oft in the stilly night,
> Ere Slumber's chain has bound me,
> Fond Memory brings the light
> Of other days around me;
> The smiles, the tears,
> Of boyhood's years,
> The words of love then spoken;
> The eyes that shone
> Now dimmed and gone.
> The cheerful hearts now broken!

Two years later, when sharing lodgings with Antoine Charbonnel, Berlioz bought a copy of Moore's *The Loves of the Angels* to increase his knowledge of the Dublin-born poet. He also loved Moore's *Irish*

Berlioz often ate his frugal meals sitting beneath this imposing equestrian statue of Henri IV.

Melodies (1807) with music by Sir John Stevenson, a collection that made Moore the national songwriter of Ireland. In 1818 Moore had visited Byron in Italy and later, in 1823, moved to Paris where he stayed for a year or two.

The frugality of Berlioz's life at this time* was a worry to some of his friends, including Augustin de Pons. But de Pons made the same mistake as Lesueur: he wrote to Dr Berlioz for help. It was a great error. At that time the doctor was under the accusing eye of his wife for allowing their son to return to Paris and so encouraging what she was convinced were dissolute ways. There was little sign of real progress in his music studies, and on top of that his was the outstanding debt. Dr Berlioz paid de Pons the six hundred francs still owing and wrote to Hector that there would be no more money from home to support his wild goose chase into the realms of music. The moment of truth had arrived. Could Berlioz support himself? Like many an

*Dr Berlioz more than once threatened to cut off Hector's allowance. He finally did it in 1826, though he restored the payments in the autumn of 1827.

30

aspiring artist he came to a firm decision to stand on his own two feet. Thus his real experience of *la vie de bohème* began in his year of decision, 1826. The summer was fading. It would have been tempting for him to return to the warmth and security of La Côte Saint-André. But it was even more tempting for a young hopeful in musical composition to stay in Paris and learn for himself at first hand what the autumn and winter in the capital held for him. Poverty? What was it Chateaubriand had written two years earlier?—'Talent sometimes owes its eventual success to the trials it has to endure.'

Yet 1826 had not been a year of complete failure. The text of *La révolution grecque* had been published in March, in August he became a full-time student at the Conservatoire, and in September he met Antoine Charbonnel, born in the same year as himself, also in La Côte Saint-André. Charbonnel was a chemistry student, and he too was wondering how to survive the coming winter in Paris. It was a happy partnership, for by sharing lodgings in the rue de la Harpe on the Left Bank, and by eating frugally, this pair of aspirants, now twenty-three, managed to face the winter and live on that 30 francs a month. Indeed, there was even some saving, since Dr Berlioz's allowance was still forthcoming.

Vert Galante, Ile de la Cité, a favourite haunt of the student Berlioz.

All the same, money was short, and in any case he had determined to make his own way, so an income was required. Accordingly, when he heard that a vaudeville theatre was opening in the rue Vivienne,

The *brasserie* Le Vaudeville now stands on the site of the old Théâtre des Nouveautés, where Berlioz sang in the chorus.

opposite the stock exchange, and needed chorus singers, he applied. As his sight reading was excellent, he was engaged at a fee of fifty francs a month, though it was not until 1 March 1827 that the first performance was given and Hector Berlioz became a professional singer at the Théâtre des Nouveautés. Had his mother known that her son was in vaudeville she would probably have died of shame. Berlioz himself was not all that proud of his new employment, and he took pains to see that his room-mate believed his journeys to the other side of Paris were undertaken to teach private pupils.

On the site of the old Théâtre des Nouveautés the Vaudeville Café now stands, opposite the Bourse des Valeurs. By a remarkable coincidence, the new Théâtre des Nouveautés in Boulevard Poissonière is almost on the site of the old Conservatoire attended by Berlioz.

32

On 5 June 1826 Carl Maria von Weber, who had been in Paris the previous February, died in London, aged only forty years. Berlioz, as we have seen, was saddened by his failure to meet Weber in person in Paris, the more so since Weber had been a strong influence in developing the romantic element in Berlioz's own emergent work. Weber's *Oberon*, commissioned for London's Covent Garden Opera House, had been a failure, for various reasons, among them an impossible 'book'. *Euryanthe* had been only a limited success in Vienna in 1823—*Der Freischütz* had appealed much more to the Germans because of its nationalistic sentiments and imagery. Weber, a cousin by marriage of Mozart, led a dissolute life, and the sickening effects of operatic failure on top of the congenital consumption from which he suffered led to his early death. A stronger soul was required to fulfil the romantic bias of his music, and it was Hector Berlioz who was to carry music on from the premises outlined in *Der Freischütz*—the expressive orchestration, the emphasis on musical drama and the daring innovations in scoring that expressed the new spirit of the Romantic movement.

But the influence of Weber on Berlioz was for the future. The immediate influence in that winter of 1826 came from his room-mate Antoine Charbonnel. Noting Hector's still active passion for Estelle Duboeuf and recognizing that his companion's love was entirely unrequited, Antoine tried to interest Hector in other girls. Could he, Antoine, be to Hector what Benvolio was to Romeo before Romeo met Juliet? Could he persuade his lovesick friend to mix with the girls of Paris and forget the unresponsive Estelle?

Harriet Smithson, the Irish actress who supplanted Estelle Duboeuf as the object of Berlioz's affections, playing in *Romeo and Juliet*.

> *Benvolio.* Be ruled by me, forget to think of her.
> *Romeo.* O teach me how I should forget to think.
> *Benvolio.* By giving liberty unto thine eyes. Examine other beauties.

Antoine would spend many an evening chasing girls ('*grisettes*'), but Hector would not join him. His heart belonged only to Estelle, despite the unhelpful fact that she herself knew nothing of it.

Romeo could think only of Rosaline, a girl who refused to return his love. When Romeo did meet Juliet, Rosaline was abruptly thrust out of his mind. Similarly, when Berlioz first saw Harriet Smithson, the Irish actress who was to bedevil his life, and his marital hopes, Estelle was immediately pushed out of his thoughts. But there the analogy ends. There was a major difference: Juliet returned Romeo's love; Harriet did not return that of Berlioz, despite the marriage vows. So poor Berlioz was no better off with his second love than with his first, even though he did manage to make a little more progress. His whole life was to be dominated by his passion for the woman of the moment, and Charbonnel despaired of his friend ever becoming patient enough to go through the process of wooing a maiden. Alas, Hector Berlioz saw, fell instantly in love, and expected his adoration to be no less instantly returned. Estelle was astonished when, late in life, she discovered that Berlioz had loved her.

Harriet Smithson feared that Berlioz was a madman when he forced his attentions on her. He became madly infatuated with her when he saw her playing Ophelia in Paris. He had no idea how to gain the confidence of a woman: he rushed in like a maniac, demanding an instant return of his own fierce passion. His parents had laughed at his childhood passion for Estelle; his friends despaired for him in his youthful passion for Harriet Smithson.

In March 1827 Berlioz found himself in possession of an income from his more or less secret work in the Nouveautés, so he bought himself a piano for 110 francs. He was not a pianist, but he could hammer out a few chords and found it useful. He completed the overture to *Les francs juges*, his first full-scale orchestral work, and followed it with the *Waverley* overture. He had learned a great deal about instrumental capabilities from his teachers and by talking with players (a trombonist at the Opéra had told him that D flat was a particularly good key for the trombone). He also learned by taking scores with him to concerts so that he could 'understand the character and tone of most of the instruments'. He wrote in his *Memoirs*: 'By continually comparing the effect achieved with the means used to obtain it I came to appreciate the subtle connection between musical expression and the technique of instrumentation; but no one had let me into the secret. I analysed the methods of those three modern masters, Beethoven, Weber and Spontini.'

Berlioz had for some time been drifting away from his first teacher, Lesueur. He found that Anton Reicha, a Bohemian composer who settled in Paris in 1808 and taught at the Conservatoire from 1818, taught him a great deal, mainly because unlike Lesueur and Cherubini, Reicha gave reason for the rules he recommended. He had studied mathematics in his youth and had been a fellow student of Beethoven in Bonn. Reicha believed that mathematics tamed his imagination to good effect, though Berlioz believed that the ability to calculate harmed the ability to create. Berlioz was not the only Reicha pupil to achieve eminence: Liszt, Gounod and César Franck also studied with him. He himself was an active composer, and his opera *Sappho*, admired by Berlioz, ran for twelve nights at the Opéra in December 1822.

In late July Berlioz had been disqualified from the Institute competition because his orchestral arrangement of the set piece, *Orpheus Torn by the Bacchantes*, was pronounced 'unplayable' by the music section panel, which included Cherubini and Lesueur. Berlioz argued that the piece was only unplayable because the pianist, Louis-Victor-Etienne Rifaut, who later became professor of accompaniment at the Conservatoire, was not good enough and that anyway it was impossible to judge orchestral music reduced to a piano score. Something of the scorn Berlioz felt towards the piano can be deduced from the following entry in the *Memoirs*: 'The piano, in short, by destroying all sense of instrumentation, places every composer on the same level.' His attitude may have in part been a result of the fact that he never really mastered the instrument. Brahms, for example, effectively reduced his own four symphonies to four-hand piano versions, whilst Liszt and Chopin would certainly not have shared Berlioz's opinion.

He had taken a fortnight's leave from the Nouveautés in the hope that by winning the Prix de Rome he would not need to go back to 'tread the boards'. His failure forced him to return to the soul-destroying work in vaudeville, much as Gustav Mahler was later condemned to 'the treadmill of the theatre' after failing to win an important competition in Vienna. Berlioz's friend Charbonnel, observing his colleague's anguish, suggested an outing on the town to buy wine and find a couple of pretty girls. But Hector, full of romantic melancholy, declined the offer and chose to spend his non-working hours alone in the lodgings. He became ill with a dangerous quinsy, and it is possible that without his medical knowledge he would have choked to death: '. . . had I not stuck a penknife down my throat and lanced the abscess that was choking me I would have died. From that moment I began to get better.'

There was genuine fatherly concern in Dr Berlioz far away in La Côte Saint-André, as secretly he admired his son's pertinacity. He worried about how Hector could survive without a steady income, and accordingly restored the former allowance. This was indeed a joyous boon to Berlioz. The senseless grind at the Nouveautés, the banal productions with titles like *Grandma's Young Man*, *The Man Who Liked Widows* and *The Little Beggar Girl* depressed him. For his father to take a step that freed him from such rubbish made Hector ecstatic. 'The sheer stupidity of the music . . . would have ended by bringing me down with cholera or turning me into a raving lunatic. Only a true musician . . . will understand what I went through.'

The euphoria restored his capacity to compose, and it was in this creative frame of mind that he saw and immediately fell in love with Harriet Smithson. This was in September 1827. He was free of the vaudeville chorus work, his allowance was newly secured from his father, he was composing and studying again, and now this wonderful glorious actress, through her grace, charm and beauty, and her portrayal of Ophelia in *Hamlet* and Juliet in *Romeo and Juliet*, had captured his fiery, romantic young heart. The effect was momentous —Smithson and Shakespeare: 'I recognized the meaning of grandeur, beauty, dramatic truth . . . The study of high dramatic music was a religion to which I devoted myself body and soul.'

At this stage in his career, instrumental music meant little to

Berlioz. He only heard the symphonies of Haydn and Mozart played by inadequate orchestras; all the same, despite the poor performances in the Paris of the 1820s, he did perceive that Beethoven was exceptional. It did not make much immediate difference; for the time being Harriet Smithson took precedence over even Beethoven in the vulnerable imaginings of his mind.

Fact and fiction merge in recording the assault of the impetuous young Berlioz on the Irish actress. Did he send so many flowers that Harriet thought him mad? Did he fling himself in the roadway so that she had to order her coachman to take a different route? Did he declare to her: 'I am your slave!'—to which she is said to have replied: 'Slavery has been abolished!' Did Antoine Charbonnel remind him that the English were a cold race, and prompt the reply: 'The lady is Irish!'? He himself records: 'I lost the power of sleep . . . I wandered aimlessly about the Paris streets . . . It was on my return from one of these wanderings (during which I looked like a man searching for his soul) that I came upon my copy of Thomas Moore's *Irish Melodies*, open at the page which begins "When he who adores thee". I wrote music to the heartrending farewell straight off. It is the song called *Elégie*.'

Berlioz did not know English. 'I could only glimpse Shakespeare darkly through the mists of Letourneur's translation'—so in 1828 he attended evening classes in English. He became an excellent reader and eventually spoke the language tolerably well.

Because Harriet had become the rage of Paris while he existed in miserable obscurity, Berlioz resolved to make himself known to her, not as a madman but to show her 'that I too was a dramatic artist'. He spent every waking hour copying the parts for the programme of music he had specially selected to prove himself to her. He saved every sou to pay the chorus and musicians. He needed a hall and chose the Conservatoire auditorium. Permission had to be obtained from the secretary of Fine Arts, M. Sosthène de la Rochefoucauld, and also from Cherubini. Wisely, Berlioz approached M. de la Rochefoucauld first; and that permission was readily granted. But Cherubini was not so co-operative, as the following altercation suggests:

'So you wish to give a concert?'

'Yes, sir.'

'For that you will 'ave to 'ave the pairmission of the Secretary of Fine Arts.'

'I have got it.'

'But—but—but—I do not agree. And—and—and I object to your 'aving the 'all.'

In the end Cherubini gave way, but he insisted that the concert be given on a Sunday, to which Berlioz agreed. In the end it took him a

Opposite:
Delacroix's vision of Faust from one of his series of lithographs.

long time to prepare this musical feast for his unsuspecting inamorata, and it was not until 26 May 1828 that the concert took place. Had he succeeded in impressing his loved one? On one plane he was rewarded; he wrote in his *Memoirs*: 'Several papers spoke enthusiastically of the concert . . . Fétis, editor of the *Revue Musicale*, said some extremely flattering things about me . . . hailing my appearance . . . as a notable event.' But had these repercussions been enough to reach Miss Smithson? Apparently not: 'Alas, I learnt later that, engrossed in her brilliant task, of me and my concert, my struggles, my success, she never heard a word.'

It was not only with women that Berlioz rushed in with this madly adoring passion that was so counter-productive. He admired several artists, among them Jean Auguste Dominique Ingres, who described some of Rossini's work as 'the music of a dishonest man', but who declared his admiration for Gluck. However, Ingres regarded Berlioz as a kind of monster, a brigand or antichrist of music. France was poverty stricken at the start of the nineteenth century and it was not until 1806 that Ingres was allowed to go to Italy to take up the scholarship awarded when he won the Prix de Rome in 1801. He remained in Italy until 1810 and during these years he painted in new genres, including nudes, of which *The Valpinçon Baigneuse* is one of the best known. His works were not well received in Paris, which is one reason why he stayed on in Italy; yet when he did return to the French capital he was accepted as the rival to Delacroix.

Eugène Delacroix was an artist not over-impressed with the romantic nationalism of the nineteenth century. He was more attracted to the ideals of the eighteenth century, and was therefore a notable bridge between the two centuries, neither forgetting the past nor being swept away by the present. It is nowadays accepted that Eugène was not the son of his legal father, Charles Delacroix, but was in fact fathered by the great French diplomat, Talleyrand. He regularly met the leading artists and intellectuals in Paris—Victor Hugo, George Sand, Chopin, Paganini, Dumas, Baudelaire, Gautier and others. Berlioz greatly admired Delacroix, the more so when he realized that the artist was a great enthusiast of literature, especially Shakespeare and Byron. Many of Delacroix's paintings came about in response to literature—in 1828 he published a series of *Faust* lithographs. He also shared Berlioz's fascination with distant countries. His visit to Morocco in 1832 inspired him for the rest of his life: the dignity of Oriental life seemed to him to be the very spirit of antiquity. He was also a gifted writer as well as a great painter. Baudelaire said that 'Delacroix was passionately in love with passion', a description that could equally be applied to Berlioz, whom some commentators have referred to as 'the Delacroix of music'.

Hector Berlioz was perceptive in his judgement of most of the great names of the eighteenth and nineteenth centuries. His opinion

A study of Berlioz in 1863 by Petit.

could be often more accurate than an artist's judgement of himself. For instance, Jean-Jacques Rousseau, who died eleven years before the French Revolution but whose writings did more than anyone else's to bring it about, could not see that his books were far superior to his so-called operas. Berlioz marvelled that this genius, who had so dramatically advertised the rights of the poor, had so effectively influenced the minds of people and directed the course of history, could think so highly of, for example, his opera *Le Devin du Village* (*The Village Magician*). Berlioz had the temerity, and the perspicacity, to write: 'Poor Rousseau! He valued his music for *The Village Magician* as highly as all the great literary works by which his name lives.' But although *Le Devin du Village* had four hundred performances after its première in 1753, Berlioz was right. Once the puerility was exposed the work died, and the last performance was given in 1829. Rousseau's outstanding work was *Le Contrat social* (1762), which was for safety published in Amsterdam and advocated that all governments should be by consent of the governed. He demanded a republic, and his claim for 'liberty, equality and fraternity' later became the battle cry of the Revolution. He also advocated that 'natural religion' should be taught in schools in place of church doctrine.

Berlioz's critical acumen made him recognize the genius of Beethoven. Most French composers of the time had no desire to see homage paid to a German. This was a general sentiment, and Berlioz had to 'drag' Lesueur to a Beethoven concert, though he was gratified that his teacher was at least honest enough to admit, after hearing the C minor symphony, that Beethoven was a composer of exceptional merit. Paris in 1828 began slowly to open its eyes and its ears to music by young 'foreign' composers. In February of that year François Antoine Haberneck, the conductor at the Opéra, founded the Société des Concerts du Conservatoire, which did invaluable work in introducing Beethoven's music to Paris. Berlioz found Haberneck wanting as a conductor but applauded the part he played in bringing out and popularizing the Beethoven symphonies. Richard Wagner was later to write that he had never heard better performances of Beethoven's symphonies than those of the Haberneck Conservatoire concerts. Berlioz records that he heard the *Eroica* on 9 and 23 March 1828 and the Fifth symphony on 13 April. On 1 November 1829 Ferdinand Hiller was soloist in the *Emperor* concerto, Haberneck again conducting, and in this concert Berlioz's own *Les francs juges* and *Waverley* overtures were included.

In June 1828 he entered for the third time the examination at the Institute, which was open to native-born or naturalized Frenchmen under the age of thirty. He won second prize, which was a gold medal and a free pass to all the opera houses. The first prize was again denied him, though he desperately wanted it since it carried with it three thousand francs per annum for five years, on condition that the holder spent the first two years at the French Academy in Rome, the third visiting Germany, and the last two in Paris. In thus having difficulty over the Prix de Rome, Berlioz was anticipating another of France's greatest composers, Maurice Ravel, whose failure to win it provoked a public scandal in 1905.

In August 1828 he spent several weeks at home in La Côte Saint-André, returning to Paris in October. He had begun writing a few articles on music, not only for money but because he used it as a weapon 'for defending the beautiful and attacking whatever seemed to me opposed to it!' True to form, he crashed madly into this new activity; but when Michaud, his editor, saw what Hector had written, he was aghast. 'All this may be true, but you've gone quite mad. I couldn't possibly publish a piece like that.' Once Berlioz realized that

The grandiose entrance of
the Opéra-Comique.

there were restrictions and limitations in journalism, he lost interest
and ever afterwards found writing a thoroughly arduous labour. He
could write music for hours at a time, but it was utter boredom to sit
down and compose an article.

He did, however, write to Harriet Smithson, but it did no good:
she did not reply and finally instructed her maid not to accept any
more letters from the impetuous and persistent young man. In an
attempt to get his name onto the same programme as hers, he
persuaded the conductor of the pit orchestra to play his *Waverley*
overture, forgetting that no one ever listened to the curtain raiser.
Anyway, Harriet remained in total ignorance of the music. It was her
last performance at the Opéra-Comique, and she left for Holland a
few days later.

By poignant chance he had taken lodgings in the rue Richlieu,
almost opposite Harriet's apartment at the corner of rue Neuve-

The rue de Richelieu; Berlioz's lodgings at number 96 placed him almost opposite Harriet's apartment in the rue Neuve-Saint-Marc.

Saint-Marc. He had apparently forgotten his Estelle: his longing for Harriet was almost 'tearing my heart out by the roots!' Today the streets are still narrow so that, even if lovers cannot hold hands, they can at least hold conversation.

Would the arrival of 1829 see an end to his unrequited love for the Shakespearean actress? Most men would have given up and looked elsewhere. But not Berlioz. He decided to write the most fantastic symphony ever. Then she *would* listen, and respond to all that he begged of her as one great dramatic artist to another.

3 Symphonie fantastique 1829-1830 in Paris

Berlioz once remarked: 'Ma vie est un roman qui m'intéresse beaucoup' ('My life is a romance* which greatly interests me'). That *'roman'* is delineated with remarkable accuracy in his music, especially during these two vital and impressionable years. The story of the *Symphonie fantastique* is almost the same as that of Berlioz's life in 1829 and the succeeding year. In fact, the film of his life in which Jean-Louis Barrault played the part of the composer was not called *'Berlioz'* but quite justifiably *Symphonie fantastique.* Nor must the sequel to the *Symphonie, Lélio, ou le Retour à la vie* ('Lélio, or the return to life') be overlooked, for it forms the second part of an integral two-part work, even if the symphonic part has justifiably become much more famous. *Lélio* is a musical self-portrait for narrator, solo singer, chorus and orchestra in the form of a 'mono-drama' set to his own words. Ideally it should follow the *symphonie* in performance but virtually never does. It is a highly eccentric piece, typical of Berlioz in many respects and in more ways than one fully representative of his temperament and overtly romantic personality.

In the *Symphonie fantastique* Berlioz's fantasized private life is brilliantly translated into orchestral terms. It remains an extraordinary work, the more so when one remembers that it was first performed within three years of the death of Beethoven. It introduced entirely new elements into the orchestral repertoire: whatever may be the final judgement on its intrinsic musical merits, the brilliance and originality of its orchestral execution can never be disputed. It owes almost equally to the classical tradition, represented primarily by Gluck, and the new Romantic spirit that had swept through Europe and of which Berlioz was one of the foremost musical exemplars. Formally, the *Symphonie fantastique* is notable for its use of the *idée fixe*, or fixed central unifying motif, the recurring theme, varied in shape and treatment but appearing in all movements, which is one of Berlioz's more obvious contributions to musical form and structure. It occurs in several of his works and represents musically the object of his particular obsession of the time;

*There is no exact equivalent in English for the French *'roman'*, which cannot be accurately translated either by 'romance' or by 'story', though it contains elements of both.
In the Pierre Boulez/CBS recording of the *Symphonie* and *Lélio*, the part of the narrator is spoken by Jean-Louis Barrault.

A poster for the film of Berlioz's life, *La Symphonie fantastique*, with Jean-Louis Barrault in the title role and (written very small) 'Musique de Hector Berlioz'!

in this case it of course represents Harriet Smithson, while in *Lélio* it represents himself. The first part of the *idée fixe* in the *symphonie* is derived from a theme in a cantata, *Herminie*, he had written in 1827. The complete *idée* in the *symphonie* runs to forty bars, though it seldom reappears in its entirety.

The first performance of the *Symphonie fantastique* took place at the Paris Conservatoire on 5 December 1830, under Haberneck's direction. Berlioz prepared elaborate programme notes that he appended to the score, insisting that they were essential to its proper comprehension. This is how they appear in the Eulenberg miniature edition:

A young musician of great sensibility and plentiful imagination, in deep despair because of hopeless love, has poisoned himself with opium. The drug is not strong enough to kill him but puts him into deep sleep with strange dreams. His sensations, emotions and memories, as they filter through his fevered brain, are transformed into musical images and ideas. The beloved one herself becomes to him a tune, a recurring theme (the *idée fixe*) which continually haunts him.

1. *Reveries, Passions.* First he remembers the weariness of the soul, that indefinable longing, that sombre melancholia and those objectless joys which he experienced before meeting his beloved. Then the explosive love which immediately inspired him, his delirious suffering, his return to tenderness, his religious consolations.

2. *A Ball.* At a ball, in the middle of a noisy brilliant fête, he finds his beloved again.

3. *In the Country.* On a summer evening in the country, he hears two shepherds calling each other with their folk melodies. The pastoral duet in such surroundings, the gentle rustle of the trees swayed by the wind, some reasons for hope which had come to his knowledge recently—all unite to fill his heart with a unique tranquillity and lend brighter colours to his fancies.

Forty bars demonstrating the *idée fixe* in the *Symphonie fantastique*. The first part comes from the cantata that was Berlioz's unsuccessful 1827 entry for the Prix de Rome. The remarkable irregularity of phrasing, which can on first hearing be disconcerting to the listener, with familiarity becomes a source of strength and delight.

Idée fixe

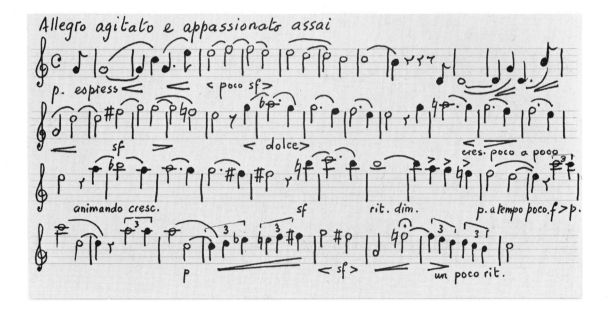

A more formal portrait of Harriet Smithson.

But his beloved appears anew, spasms contract his heart, and he is filled with dark premonition. What if she proved faithless? Only one of the shepherds resumes his rustic tune. The sun sets. Far away there is a rumble of thunder—solitude—silence.

4. *March to the Scaffold.* He dreams he has killed his loved one, that he is condemned to death and led to his execution. A march, now gloomy yet ferocious, now solemn yet brilliant, accompanies the procession. Noisy outbursts are followed without pause by the heavy sound of marching footsteps. Finally, like a last thought of love, the *idée fixe* briefly appears, to be cut off by the fall of an axe.

5. *Dream of a Witches' Sabbath.* He sees himself at a Witches' Sabbath, surrounded by a fearful crowd of spectres, sorcerers, and monsters of every kind, united for his burial. Unearthly sounds, groans, shrieks of laughter, distant cries, to which others seem to respond! The melody of his beloved is heard, but it has lost its character of nobility and reserve. It is now an ignoble dance tune, trivial and grotesque. It is she who comes to the Sabbath! A shout of joy greets her arrival. She joins the diabolical orgy. The funeral knell, burlesque of the *Dies Irae.* Dance of the Witches. The dance and the *Dies Irae* combine.

It will be seen that not all his thoughts of the beloved were sweet and tender. Indeed, he was at the time having bouts of revulsion against Harriet and her treatment (real or imagined) of him. Hence the Hieronymus Bosch-like vision of the Witches' Sabbath, and the vision of himself as the murderer of the faithless loved one and his consequent leading off to the scaffold, an idea that greatly appealed to the romantic imagination but would hardly astonish a contemporary post-Freud psychologist.

Although Berlioz remained obsessed with Harriet Smithson he had not completely forgotten Estelle. The theme played by the first violins at the start of the Largo introduction to the first movement, 'Reveries, Passions', makes use of a tune written in 1817 during the time of his Meylan passion for the pretty girl in pink boots. He had burned the actual manuscript before he left for Paris, but the music remained lodged in his memory. This theme was 'exactly right for a young heart caught in the toils of hopeless love'. Something of his attitude towards women can be gleaned from some conversations he had with a porter at the Institute, a M. Pingard, an ex-sailor. These conversations also re-emphasize Berlioz's fascination with distant lands and exotic places, as well as his irritation at coming only second in the Institute's annual competition. 'I questioned him [Pingard] closely about Javanese women, whose love is said to be fatal to Europeans.' Pingard laughed at this myth, pointing out that because he himself was still alive it *must* be untrue. 'One day at the Cape of Good Hope I was waiting for a little negress. She'd agreed to meet me on the shore . . .'

'Quite, quite!' Berlioz interrupted, not wishing to hear the more salacious details. He had the pre-Christian adoration of 'Woman', the beautiful marble statue, the perfect one, whose nose would not run if she had a cold, whose body would not perspire in the extreme heat, or produce goose-pimples in the cold. He clung to this Grecian vision of woman on a pedestal, a vision to be adored, and did not want it destroyed. He could open his eyes to the perfections of Beethoven and the imperfections of Rossini in a totally rational manner, but he did not want to be rational in his worship of 'Woman'. Just as he had refused Antoine Charbonnel's invitations to chase after girls as a relaxation from work, now he stopped Pingard's obviously gloating recollections of clandestine meetings on the shore. In both cases he stepped away from a situation where 'Woman' would be revealed as less than perfect. It was a romantic attitude typical of that period. 'Go on about Levaillant!' he urged Pingard, prompting the porter to change the subject and talk about something and somebody more interesting. Levaillant was a famous explorer, and Berlioz was much more willing to hear about his exploits.

He also confided to Pingard his disappointment about not winning first prize in the Institute competition. Pingard told him the truth:

You were only two votes short of the first prize. You don't know what a damned bazaar it is. They get together and bargain over the votes; they even sell them.

This insight into the judging habits in the matter of the Prix de Rome only confirmed Berlioz's own suspicions; but it stood him in good stead when he did finally win in the following year, 1830. His eyes were further opened by Boïeldieu, a composer of over thirty operas, who took an active interest in Berlioz's musical upbringing. It was 2 August 1829, the day after the jury had decided not to award a first prize.

'My dear boy, what have you done?'
'I assure you, sir, I did my best.'
'You should not have done your best. Your best is the enemy of the good. You know I like soothing music.'
'Sir, it is a little difficult to write soothing music for an Egyptian queen who has been bitten by a poisonous snake and is dying a painful death in an agony of remorse.'
'Oh, I know you have an answer—you always have. But that proves nothing. It is always possible to be graceful.'
'Gladiators could die gracefully, but not Cleopatra. She hadn't the knack —it was not her way. Besides, she wasn't dying in public.'
'You exaggerate. We were not asking you to make her sing a quadrille . . .'

And more along the same lines. Berlioz always had the obstinate honesty of the true artist, refusing to compromise even if it was in his interests so to do. But he could still be artful—and listen. 'Ah, well, you've always got an answer, haven't you?' Boïeldieu concluded. 'Goodbye, take this lesson to heart and be more sensible next year!'

He did: the combined advice of the professor and the porter was taken to heart and at his next attempt Berlioz was successful.

The cause of the trouble had been the cantata he had written on the set theme of *Cleopatra After the Battle of Actium*, when she clasps the asp to her bosom and dies. Berlioz wrote for this occasion his remarkable and imaginative cantata *La mort de Cléopâtre*, a striking piece that, if it does little in the way of presaging the startling originalities of the *Symphonie fantastique*, contains some fine dramatic declamation and some music for the 'Grand Pharaohs' which is as good and powerful as Boïeldieu's objection to it suggests. Berlioz also introduced a tune he was later to use to notable effect in his opera *Benvenuto Cellini*.

In 1830 he used his common sense when he wrote his entry for the Prix de Rome. It was his fifth attempt, and on 21 August he heard that he had been awarded first prize. It meant an annuity of one thousand crowns, free entry to every opera house, and financial independence for the next five years. He had learned something at least about how to write music that pleased his adjudicators.

But no one could advise him on women. He might have been wiser to adopt the philosophy of Sir Thomas Beecham, who would not combine women and music. As he put it: 'If they're ugly they put me off, and if they're pretty they put the orchestra players off!'

Having transferred his adoration from Estelle Duboeuf to Harriet Smithson, Berlioz could not have been expected to perform another volte-face, especially in 1830, the year of the Harriet-inspired *Symphonie fantastique*, even though part of that composition was composed in reaction against Harriet's obstinate lack of response to his advances. That is certainly what Berlioz's friend the German pianist–composer Ferdinand Hiller thought. Hiller was concerned about Hector's infatuation with the Shakespearean actress; but it seems that he knew as little about women as the love-lorn Berlioz. Hiller had a young girlfriend, Camille Moke, who later became one of the most distinguished pianists of the nineteenth century. He spoke to Camille about his friend's mad infatuation, adding (foolishly): 'I'd never be jealous of him, for it is certain he will never fall in love with you!'

Camille, however, became determined to prove her trusting admirer wrong. At the time Berlioz was teaching the guitar at the girls' boarding school of Madame d'Aubré in the rue Harlay-Marais, where Camille taught the piano. She told Berlioz that Hiller was fond of her but that she did not return his affection; and it was not long before the teenage pianist had the ardent Hector kneeling metaphorically if not literally at her feet. He later wrote in recollection, if not in tranquillity, 'I yielded and let myself find consolation for all my sorrows in a new passion, into which I threw myself with an enthusiasm not at all surprising when one considers

Camille Moke, who to prove her current admirer wrong set out to capture Berlioz's affections—and became engaged to him.

my age [he was twenty-seven] and ardent disposition and the eighteen years and maddening beauty of Mlle Moke.'

It was a quick and passionate affair. Berlioz wrote in his *Memoirs*: 'If I were to describe the whole affair and the incredible incidents of every kind to which it gave rise, the reader would no doubt be entertained in an unexpected and interesting fashion. But, as I have stated before, I am not writing confessions. Suffice it to say that Mlle M . . . set my senses on fire till all the devils of hell danced in my veins. Poor Hiller when I told him the truth, as I felt I had to, wept bitterly at first. Then, realizing that I had not fundamentally been guilty of treachery towards him, he put a brave and dignified face on it, clasped my hand convulsively, wished me every joy, and left for Frankfurt.'

It would appear, from the way he confesses that Camille made 'all the devils of hell' dance within him and the way in which he cast Harriet into the Witches' Cauldron as a kind of pennance for sins committed or imagined, that Berlioz had a fair working knowledge of Hell. If only, now, the two young men, Hiller and Berlioz, could have known how Camille's mind worked, or more to the point how the mind of her mother worked, they might not have indulged in such noble and histrionic recriminations. On 23 August Berlioz wrote:

I have won the Prix de Rome . . . even her mother, who does not look too favourably on our love, was touched to tears. (That wretched Smithson girl is still here.)

Whereas a few months previously Berlioz would have sworn that his success was due to the inspiration of Harriet, now, true to the vagaries of a love-sick mind, Camille was given all the credit. On 24 July he had written:

All that love offers is most tender and delicate, I have from Camille. My enchanting sylph, my Ariel, my life, seems to love me more than ever: as for me, her mother keeps on saying that if she had read in a novel the description of love like mine she would not believe it true.

The Revolution of 1830 broke out in July. It caused much disturbance, but nothing could deflect Berlioz from work on the *Symphonie fantastique*.

I dashed off the final pages of my orchestral score to the sound of stray bullets coming over the roofs and pattering on the wall outside my window.

The 'dashing off' was possible because he drew so heavily on previous compositions, both published and unpublished. The literary schema seemed inevitable at that period: such expression was the essence of the Romantic movement. Anyway Berlioz, a great lover of literature, had a flair for words and, like the Romantic movement itself, needed to explain himself publicly. Later in his life

49

Berlioz tried to remove the 'literary scaffolding' in the hope that the symphony could stand on musical content alone; and indeed, the test of time has proved the *Symphonie fantastique* to be a musical masterpiece.

The labour of its composition, however, was long and arduous, through 1829 and 1830. The slow movement, the 'Scène au champs', took nearly a month to write, though Berlioz claimed that the 'Marche au sulplice' took only a night. (But that came mainly from his unfinished opera *Les francs juges* with the *idée fixe* tacked onto the end.)

The previous 1 November Berlioz had given a concert at the Conservatoire, with a programme that included the cantata *Huit Scènes de Faust* ('Eight Scenes from Faust'), written specifically for Harriet Smithson. It made little impression at the time, but eighteen years later, in an expanded version known as *La Damnation de Faust*, it became a favourite all over Europe, being frequently encored in places as far apart and widely differing as St Petersburg, Moscow, Berlin, London and Paris. It is now recognized as one of its composer's most original works.

But disaster struck him again in May 1830 when he tried to arrange a rehearsal of the *Symphonie fantastique* at the Théâtre des Nouveautes. It was absolute chaos. There was not nearly enough room for the 130 musicians, no music stands, and there was noise and quarrelling everywhere. He tried to rehearse the 'Ball' and the 'March', but the directors of the theatre recoiled in horror, so in the end the concert never took place.

Berlioz took such setbacks in his stride. 'Why?' he asked, blaming only himself. 'What had gone wrong?' From such adversities he gained in practical wisdom. Later he could write:

The extreme care which I now take over practical details of concert-giving dates from then. I know too well what disasters the least negligence in this respect can lead to.

In November 1830 he completed the dramatic fantasy, *The Tempest*, and Lubbert, Director at the Opéra between 1827 and 1831, agreed to put the production on. (This Opéra building has disappeared: the present Opéra is on a different site.) Much to Berlioz's relief the operatic rehearsals went well and he was encouraged to hope for a triumph on the opening night. Unfortunately, an hour before the doors opened there *was* a tempest. Berlioz did not appreciate the joke.

A mighty cloudburst turned the streets into veritable rivers and lakes; all traffic, wheeled or on foot, became virtually impossible . . . just when my own Tempest was supposed to be raging, the Opéra was almost deserted. Two or three hundred people at the most were there, performers included. All that effort 'down the drain'!

Opposite:
Two views of the reconstructed concert hall of the Conservatoire, restored to the splendour of Berlioz's day where his music was first performed 150 years ago.

50

A Pleyel piano, made by the company run by Berlioz's rival for Camille Moke, Camille Pleyel. This particular piano belonged to Bizet.

In December 1830 the unsuspecting, passionately trusting Berlioz became engaged to Camille, though the German mother of the bride-to-be set Easter 1832 as the date for the wedding. This shrewd businesswoman, who had opened a Dutch lingerie shop in the Faubourg Montmartre when her Belgian husband lost his money in speculation, was out to make the best marriage possible for her beautiful and musically talented daughter. Berlioz was a 'possible'. His prospects might be uncertain but at least he was heir to a sizeable estate. He had won the Prix de Rome, and his *Symphonie fantastique* had been successful. It was certainly worthwhile letting her daughter exchange rings with the young composer, so long as she played for safety by choosing a wedding date conveniently far ahead. Berlioz was not the only contestant for Camille's hand. His rival was Camille Pleyel, a pianomaker with an apparently booming business, since pianos were selling well, largely thanks to the popularity of pianist–composers such as Chopin and Liszt. The other piano player, Ferdinand Hiller, had removed himself from the list of Camille Moke's admirers. Berlioz was, in any case about to depart for Italy. Yes, reasoned the canny mother, let the engagement go ahead.

Poor Berlioz. How little he knew of the female mind!

As 1831 approached his world at last began to look rosy, warm, successful, and charged with potential happiness. He did not want to go to Italy, leaving his beautiful young fiancée in Paris; but he would return to claim his bride, and to build a glittering future career to follow the success of his great *Symphonie fantastique*. He had used the argument that the Italian climate would be injurious to someone of his highly strung disposition as a delaying tactic to enable him to stay in Paris with Camille; but his earnest request to the Minister of the Interior for a dispensation had not been heeded. He would lose face now if he refused to accept the prize he had won after so much effort and so many attempts; nor would it do his future any good. So many things seemed to be going right for him, including his newly formed friendship with the nineteen-year-old Liszt, that it must have seemed nonsensical to do anything that might jeopardize it.

Before leaving Berlioz decided to give a second concert at the Conservatoire, to include the *Symphonie fantastique* and his cantata *La mort de Sardanapale*, the finale of which had come to grief at the Institute prizegiving in October.

On the day before the concert Liszt called on me. It was our first meeting . . . We felt an immediate affinity, and from that moment our friendship has grown ever closer and stronger. He came to the concert and was conspicuous for the warmth of his applause and generally enthusiastic behaviour.

This concert took place on 5 December and also included the overture *Les francs juges, Chante sacré*, and *Chant guerrier* from 'Neuf mélodies'. (The same evening, at the Opéra, Harriet Smithson played the mute role of Fenella in an act from Auber's *La Muette de Portici*.) After the concert, as Berlioz wrote to his father, 'Liszt literally dragged me off to have dinner at his house and overwhelmed me with the vigour of his enthusiasm.'

He was now ready to leave for Italy at last; but his *Memoirs* contain the almost inevitable jibe at Cherubini:

'So you are leaving for Italy?' he said.
'Yes, sir.'
'Your name will no longer be on the regeester of Conservatoire students; your studies are at an end. But I theenk you ought to 'ave come and see me before goeeing. One does not go out of the Conservatoire as if it were a stable.'
I nearly replied, 'Why not, since we are treated like horses?' but I had the sense not to.

Franz Liszt, whose support and approval of Berlioz's work led to a long friendship.

Donald Tovey, in his *Essays in Musical Analysis* (Volume IV), writes of the antipathy between Berlioz and Cherubini: 'You have only to read Berlioz's own account of his diplomatic triumphs over Cherubini to see how low human nature can sink, when an ill-bred younger artist gets his chance of scoring off a disappointed old one.' At least Berlioz, on the eve of his departure, had the grace to allow Cherubini the last word.

Paris, 12 December 1830
I leave Paris at the beginning of January. My marriage is fixed for Easter 1832, on condition that I do not lose my pension, and that I go to Italy for a year. My blessed symphony has done the deed and won this condition from Camille's mother . . . oh, I am in a state of intoxication! Since she heard my *Witches' Sabbath*, Camille calls me her 'Lucifer', her 'dear Satan' . . .

Berlioz was far from well and he spent a month at home in La Côte Saint-André. His parents were now proud of their son's achievements and received him with much warmth and affection, a reconciliation that augured well for his stay in Italy. Though he received at least one letter from Camille, he also received one from his trusted friend Hiller, warning him that Camille's attitude and behaviour in Paris were not all that one might expect of a young lady engaged to be married. Berlioz sensed the truth in Hiller's warning and it did nothing to cheer him on his way.

I bent my steps towards Italy, alone and somewhat dejected.

4 Hector in Italy 1831-1832

When Lord Byron sailed from Falmouth in 1809 he collected material for his autobiographical *Childe Harold's Pilgrimage*, a 'travel' poem in Spenserian stanzas. The first two Cantos were published in 1812, and according to Thomas Moore this was the occasion that caused Byron to remark: 'I awoke one morning and found myself famous.' When Berlioz sailed from Marseilles in 1831, more than twenty years later, he too collected material for a kind of auto-biographical work, his second 'symphony', *Harold en Italie*, which he finally completed in 1834.

Many references have been made to the alleged connection between the Byronic hero and Berlioz's composition. There obviously was some connection in Berlioz's mind, hence the adoption of the title and the clear reference to Byron's Harold. But the link is otherwise pretty tenuous. As Donald Tovey wrote:

There are excellent reasons for reading *Childe Harold's Pilgrimage*. But among them I cannot find any that concern Berlioz and this symphony, except for the jejune value of the discovery that no definite elements of Byron's poem have penetrated the impregnable fortress of Berlioz's encyclo-paedic inattention.

Tovey then went on to observe, with metaphysical acumen, '. . . there is a B in Byron and a B in Berlioz . . .'

One may ask what in fact attracted Berlioz to Byron? The immediate and obvious answer is that both represented, at two or three decades remove, the innermost spirit of Romanticism. Of all the English Romantic poets, Byron was the best known and most influential in Europe. Together with the novels of Walter Scott, which brought to the European imagination the wild and romantic history and landscape of Scotland, and the rediscovery of Shake-speare, the poetry of Byron and his romantic life and death made the most considerable impact on the Continent. Shelley had lived in Italy and Keats died in Rome, but it was Byron who most vividly caught the European spirit of the Romantic Revival. As Matthew Arnold wrote of Byron after his death:

He taught us little: but our soul
Had *felt* him like the thunder's roll.

It is possible that Byron's lifestyle appealed to Berlioz as much as his poetry. When he sailed from Marseilles Byron was very much on

Byron in Italy, where he collected material for *Childe Harold's Pilgrimage.*

his mind, if only because one of the sailors, a Venetian, claimed to have been in charge of the corvette that carried the poet down the Adriatic coast and through the Greek islands. Berlioz records in his *Memoirs*:

He described in minute detail the glittering uniform which Byron had insisted on wearing and the orgies they took part in together; he made a great point of the tribute which the celebrated traveller had paid to his daring. In the middle of a storm Byron had invited him to his cabin for a game of écarté. The captain, rather than decline the invitation, left the bridge and went below. The game had begun when the ship gave a violent lurch, and the card players were sent flying.

'Pick up the cards and go on,' cried Byron.

'With pleasure, my lord.'

'Captain, you're a brave fellow.'

It is quite possible there was not a word of truth in it; but one must admit that the gold-lace uniform and the game of écarté are very much in character with the author of *Lara*. Beside, the narrator did not have enough wit to invent such convincing local colour; and I was much too pleased at meeting someone who had been with Childe Harold on his pilgrimage not to believe it all implicitly.

There was so much about Byron that Berlioz could admire—his success with women, for example, where Berlioz's own record was pathetic. His first love, Estelle Duboeuf, had been totally unaware of his feelings for her; Harriet Smithson had considered him mad and would have nothing to do with him, while his third love, Camille Moke, had returned his passion but left him with a sickening sense that she was about to jilt him. Although Byron's first love, Mary Duff, had never been more than a platonic relationship, since he was only eight at the time, and although his first serious love, Mary Chaworth, married someone else, after that it was a Casanova-like list of conquests. In 1807 he kept a girl in his room disguised as a page; later, Lady Caroline Lamb, wife of a prominent politician and one of Byron's more notorious mistresses, also disguised herself as a page and stayed in Byron's rooms.

Again, Berlioz dreamed of far-off lands, whereas Byron's adventurous spirit had taken him to many exotic places, including Seville, Gibraltar, Sardinia, Malta (where his amorous attentions to the wife of the local governor almost led to a duel), Albania (where he met the notorious Ali Pasha), Athens (where his landlady's three daughters, Mariana, Katinka and Theresa, occupied much of his time), Smyrna, Troy and Sestos where, in 1809, Byron made his famous swim across the Hellespont to Abydos, thus emulating Leander.

Berlioz had been broken hearted by his mother's curse when he left for Paris; Byron too had mother trouble, but the poet rose above it: 'The more I see of her the more my dislike augments. I have never been so *scurrilously* and *violently* abused by any person, as by that woman, whom I think I am to call mother . . .'

A bust of Napoleon, surrounded by the emblems of laurel and oak, with whom Byron was compared.

Berlioz kept religion at a distance; so did Byron. The poet claimed that, even at the age of five, religion filled him with gloom and pessimism. His early introduction to the Cain and Abel story is referred to in *Childe Harold*:

> . . . life abhoring gloom
> Wrote on his faded brow curst Cain's unresting doom.

Berlioz admired Napoleon: Byron in his day was likened to the great French leader. He:

lived and loved with wild extravagance . . . flung himself into the cause of liberty and died a hero in the eyes of all Europe, and was compared at his death with Napoleon. Byron and Napoleon, men said, were the two greatest men of the century; the comparison was not inapt, for as Napoleon remoulded Europe, so Byron gave it a new pattern to its literature.

Derek Parker in his book on Byron wrote:

In Europe the effect of Byron's death was greater (and perhaps more lasting) than in England. Many French newspapers remarked that the two greatest men of the century, Napoleon and Byron, had disappeared at almost the same time. As a myth, his influence on the younger generation of Frenchmen was enormous.

Byron died at Missolonghi, Greece, in April 1824, at the age of thirty-six, complaining to the end that the doctors would kill him if they kept on draining off his blood. The British Government refused him burial in Westminster Abbey, so when the body arrived in England on 5 July it was taken to Nottingham, passing the home of Lady Caroline Lamb. She asked her husband whose funeral it was, but he would not answer. In 1969 a Byron memorial stone was unveiled in Westminster Abbey, almost a hundred and fifty years after his death, and appropriately in the centenary year of Berlioz.

Berlioz himself was an involuntary revolutionary. How could he not be moved by Byron's stirring words in *Childe Harold*, written when the poet had toured the sacred battlefield of Waterloo?—

> Stop!—for thy tread is on an Empire's dust!
> An Earthquake's spoil is sepulchred below!
> Is the spot mark'd with no colossal bust?
> Nor column trophied for triumphal show?
> None; but the moral's truth tells simpler so,
> As the ground was before, thus let it be;—
> How that red rain hath made the harvest grow!
> And is this all the world has gain'd by thee
> Thou first and last of fields! King-making victory?

These lines from the third Canto were written in 1816, when Byron was staying at 51 rue Ducale, Brussels, having fled his creditors. He had ridden over the plain of Waterloo on horseback, whereas Victor Hugo, for the Waterloo chapter in *Les Misérables*, stayed in comfort at the Hôtel des Colonnes. Byron had a luxurious coach built, a replica of Napoleon's, but when he was pressed for payment the poet lord abruptly left. He wrote the fourth and last Canto of *Childe Harold* in 1817 while he was living in Venice with his new mistress, the Countess Guiccioli, and her compliant husband.

Thus, although there was little direct connection in either incident or locality between the two Harolds, there was much that Berlioz could contemplate and admire in Byron the man, who had inherited a title at the age of ten and thus became eligible as a member of the House of Lords. No wonder that when the storm-tossed Sardinian brig finally landed him in Italy, at Leghorn, the young student-composer's mind was very much concentrated on the English poet.

Once landed, Berlioz made his way to the Villa Medici, the Italian home of the students of the French Academy. The Villa had been built in 1557, with a wing added by Michelangelo. It stood on the slope of Pincian Hill overlooking Rome, affording a magnificent view. On his second stay at the Academy he met Mendelssohn. Perhaps harbouring thoughts of Byron's *Sardanapalus* or Delacroix's painting *The Death of Sardanapalus*, Berlioz spoke with Mendelssohn about his own *La mort de Sardanapale*. The two young composers also mentioned the suitability of the Queen Mab speech ('O then I see Queen Mab hath been with you, She is the fairies' midwife, and she comes in shape no bigger than an agate stone . . .') as an inspiration for music, as indeed it did become when Berlioz wrote his *Romeo et Juliette*, a work of sublime beauty in a form Berlioz made particularly his own; though called a 'symphony' it is not that, nor is it opera or cantata but a kind of dramatic cantata evolved in part from Berlioz's dissatisfaction with current operatic forms, in part from his own specific sense of the relationship between music and drama.

Throughout March 1831 he was ill with worry as he waited for news from Camille. The suspense became too much for him and, despite a warning that his name would be removed from the register of students, he left Rome on 1 April. When he reached Florence some mail was handed to him, and a letter from Mme Moke informed him that Camille had married M. Pleyel. His reaction was typically melodramatic:

Two tears of rage started from my eyes. In that instant I knew my course: it was to go at once to Paris and there kill without compunction two guilty women and one guilty man.

Although he was fifty-three, Camille Pleyel was a very eligible bachelor. A creditable composer and pianist, he came, like the Érard family, his rivals as piano makers, from Strassburg, and although there was Pleyel-Érard rivalry, it only served to spur the respective firms to greater efforts and higher standards. There were plenty of buyers for good pianos, so there was room for healthy competition. (Exactly a hundred years later, the two firms amalgamated.)

So Camille Pleyel had assets which Berlioz, in the eyes of his prospective mother-in-law, could not hope to match. The modest living quarters of student Berlioz could ill stand comparison with the grand living quarters of the Pleyel family. A prosperous businessman about to become the head of the firm Pleyel & Co. was a much better prospect than the seemingly eccentric composer. The beautiful teenage piano prodigy needed little persuasion to opt for the luxury of Boulogne rather than the poverty of either the Left Bank or the modest quarters in the rue St Marc or the rue Richelieu, which was about all Berlioz could afford at the time. In the circumstances, Camille and her mother felt that a letter to Berlioz informing him of the termination of the engagement was all that was required. In that, however, they were to be proved somewhat optimistic. They reckoned without the rage such a communication would provoke, a rage so insane that, as he himself noted, he immediately began to plot their deaths, which were to be followed by his own suicide.

It is probably fortunate that in those days there were no fast trains, let alone jet aircraft, to rush him and his rage from Florence to Paris. If there had been it is possible that the two ladies might not have lived long enough to walk the boulevards with the ageing Camille Pleyel. It is well documented how Berlioz bought pistols and women's clothing for his disguise, and hired a stagecoach to take him on his murderous journey to Paris. Luckily, stagecoach travel took

A stagecoach of the kind that Berlioz would have used when travelling.

time, especially in mountainous country—at least, time enough for the hot-headed young man to cool off and calm down.

On returning to Rome he was accepted back into the Villa Medici, in early June. A letter to his friend Humbert Ferrand, written on either 10 or 11 May, shows that although he had given up thoughts of triple murder and suicide, he was still simmering:

Yes, Camille is married to Pleyel. I am now glad of it. From it I have just learnt the danger I have escaped. What baseness, what insensibility, almost the sublimity of wickedness, if sublimity can ally itself with *ignobility*—(a new word, and a perfect one, which I have stolen from you).

PS. My *repertoire* has just been increased by a new overture. Yesterday I finished the one to Shakespeare's *King Lear*.

The character of Lear, an old king deceived by two women, his own daughters Goneril and Regan, no doubt appealed particularly to Berlioz at this time. To Goneril the King raged: 'Degenerate bastard, I'll not trouble thee!'; and the outraged father goes on to see his second daughter, who also scorns him—

> You see me here, you gods, a poor old man,
> As full of grief as age, wretched in both.
> If it be you that stirs these daughters' hearts
> Against their father, fool me not so much
> To bear it tamely; touch me with noble anger,
> And let not women's weapons, water-drops,
> Stain my man's cheeks. No, you unnatural hags,
> I will have such revenges on you both
> That all the world—I will do such things—
> What they are yet I know not, but they shall be
> The terrors of the earth! You think I'll weep;
> No, I'll not weep.

The tone is familiar; it seems in some way to fit in with the character of Hector Berlioz. It was not only his symphony that was *fantastique*; he was in many respects a fantastic character, one who stood out in any company, and to the reactionary French musical establishment, frequently a sore thumb. It would have been remarkable if he had not planned such things as would be 'the terrors of the earth'.

Had Berlioz learnt anything from this shattering end to his dreams of love and life with Camille Moke? There was, indeed, a marked change in his attitude towards women. It is not necessary to go into the sultry details of his amorous adventures, except where they impinge directly on his public life, as in the case of his first and second wives; but one letter does serve to indicate the change:

London. 10 November 1847. To cellist Tajan-Rogé.

. . . as I am in the confidential vein, would you believe that I let myself in for a love affair at Petersburg as genuine as it was absurd with one of your chorus girls? . . . what a number of walks we took together in the outlying parts of Petersburg and into the country, from nine to eleven at night! . . . I was really ill at Berlin at not finding a letter there from her. She had promised to write. Her fiancé must certainly be back by this time.

The girl is believed to have been Rosina Stoltz, a singer at the Paris Opéra who wielded great power over the selection of singers during Pillet's regime between 1841 and 1847. She turned against Berlioz when he suggested in *Débats* that she was putting on too much weight to play solo parts. After she left Paris she married in quick succession a baron, a duke and a prince.

On the way back to Rome Berlioz sketched the monologues for *Lélio*. His new friend Horace Vernet, painter and Director of the French Academy in Rome from 1828 to 1863, pointed out that 'work and art are two sovereign remedies for an afflicted mind'. Berlioz found solace in a tender friendship with Vernet's daughter Louise.

He found further diversion reading Byron. 'I followed the Corsair across the seas on his audacious journeys. I adored the extraordinary nature of the man . . .'* He also loved to escape to the mountains behind Rome, to the villages and in particular to Subiaco, several miles from Tivoli in the Papal States. He was popular as a guitar player, too, and frequently led groups of young Italians and Academy students in open-air singing. (One of his guitars, a Grobert made in Paris, can be seen in the Conservatoire de Musique in Paris.) He joined in the inevitable roisterings that have always been a feature of student life the world over. He writes of an 'amusing but unprintable scandal in the little town of Ciprano', and also from his *Memoirs* we have an amusing incident which can hardly have been exceptional, let alone unique—

At last some signs of life at the Academy. We have to thank our friend L---. His terror is comical to behold. It seems he has been caught by Vernet's Italian footman in the act of making love to the man's wife, and lives in constant fear of being murdered. He daren't leave his room. At mealtimes we go in a body and escort him to the refectory. He imagines he sees knives gleaming in every corner of the palace. He's wasting away; has turned pale, then yellow, and now a delicate shade of blue. The other day at lunch Delanoie greeted him with this charming remark: 'Well, my poor friend, still suffering from domestic trouble?'

The mot has become famous, and is much quoted.

L—— was apparently a great seducer of housemaids, and advocated a sure method of success with them: 'Always look sad, and wear white trousers.'

Although Berlioz's stay at the Academy was one of personal

*Much as he enjoyed reading Byron and this particular poem, his own overture *Le Corsaire* was based not on Byron but on James Fennimore Cooper's novel *The Red Rover* (French title *Le Corsaire rouge*), though no doubt Byron came at least subconsciously into it.

development rather than industry, he did compose some pieces, notably the *Rob Roy* overture of 1832 which was performed in Paris the next year, though Berlioz did not like it and destroyed the score after the concert. He also rewrote the 'Scènes aux champs' movement of the *Symphonie fantastique*, inspired now by walks near the Villa Borghese, wrote the 'Chant de Bonheur' for the monodrama *Lélio*, and, prompted by a visit to Subiaco in February 1832, composed a song, *La Captive*, a setting of a poem from Victor Hugo's *Orientales* that became unexpectedly popular. Louise Vernet liked to sing it, especially at the weekly Thursday receptions at the Academy where her father encouraged the students to be merry and make music. Berlioz, too, loved the song: 'To my mind it is one of the most colourful I have written.' Also during this period he wrote *Méditation religieuse*, a six-part cantata with orchestral accompaniment to words by Thomas Moore ('The world is all a fleeting show'), which forms the first number of his Op. 18, *Tristia*. To please the academicians in Paris he sent back, tongue in cheek, a Resurrexit that he had written before he won the Prix de Rome, but which the eminent musical scholars in Paris took as evidence of the beneficial effects of his Roman studies.

Horace Vernet gave him special dispensation to leave Rome six months before the end of the statutory two years, so he arrived home in Paris on 7 November 1832, to find much changed. The tradition of Gluck which had held the stage up to Berlioz's departure for Rome appears to have been replaced by that of Meyerbeer following the triumph of *Robert le diable* in 1831. It was a musical shift that Berlioz deplored. In addition, he found Cherubini aged and enfeebled.

His old apartment in the rue Richelieu was taken, so he moved into the house opposite, 1 rue Neuve-Saint-Marc. Alas, this was the apartment recently occupied by Harriet Smithson, who was back in Paris and currently living in the rue de Rivoli: her Shakespearean company was due to open at the Théâtre Italien on 21 November 1832. He asked the housekeeper what had become of Miss Smithson, and she told him that the actress had been staying in the same room he himself now occupied. Berlioz was thunderstruck.

I stood aghast . . . It was fate . . . We had just missed meeting in the same house; I had taken the apartment that she had left the previous evening . . . I had come to Paris to have my new work (the monodrama) performed. If I went to the English theatre and saw her again before I had given my concert, the old delirium tremens would inevitably seize me. As before, I would lose all independence of will and be incapable of attention and concentrated effort which the enterprise demanded. Let me first give my concert. Afterwards I would see her, whether as Ophelia or as Juliet, even if it killed me; I would give myself up to the destiny which seemed to pursue me, and not struggle any more.

5 Berlioz in Paris

If we look at the specially drawn 'Berlioz in Paris' street map, we can see that the composer began his life in Paris at the bottom of the map and finished it at the top. In all he had twelve addresses in Paris between his arrival in 1821 and his death forty-eight years later. His first Paris address was on the Left Bank, that is in the southern part of the city; his grave is in the Cimetière de Montmartre, situated in the northern part.

It is fitting to pause for a moment at this point in the Berlioz *roman* to take note of the direct relationship between France's foremost composer and France's capital city. The relationship was always close; it was also varied, both in locality and in the line of fortune. It had, too, a number of important historical associations.

In November 1821, when he began his osteological studies in company with his cousin Alphonse Robert, the two young men lodged at 104 rue Saint-Jacques. The Hospice de la Pitié and the Jardin des Plantes, where some of the medical lectures were given, are nearby. People of wealth in that district lived in the Boulevard Saint-Germain, which runs parallel with the Seine. The students lodged in the narrow, dimly lit passages leading to the river. Flooding was a regular hazard in a number of these streets. Rue Saint-Jacques runs from Boulevard de Port Royal, northwards through the Sorbonne University to the Seine, where a bridge, the Petit Pont, links it to the Ile de la Cité, with the cathedral of Notre Dame to the right. The exact position of Berlioz's lodging is difficult to locate as several renumberings have taken place since he lived there. Records show that his first number was 104, which became 79, but extensive rebuilding in the area makes positive identification almost impossible.

In 1795 Paris was divided into twelve administrative divisions (*arrondissements*) and in 1860 an outer ring was added, bringing the number to twenty divisions. As an old map of the city shows, rue Saint-Jacques has not had its actual position altered. The present number 269 is the Schola Cantorum, 'Ecole Superieur de Musique, de Danse, d'Art Dramatique', founded in 1894 by Vincent d'Indy and Charles Bordes to restore the standing and quality of church music. Berlioz lived in this long narrow winding street until June 1824. He made excursions north of the river in 1822, notably to the library of the Conservatoire de Musique, situated in those days

BERLIOZ IN PARIS

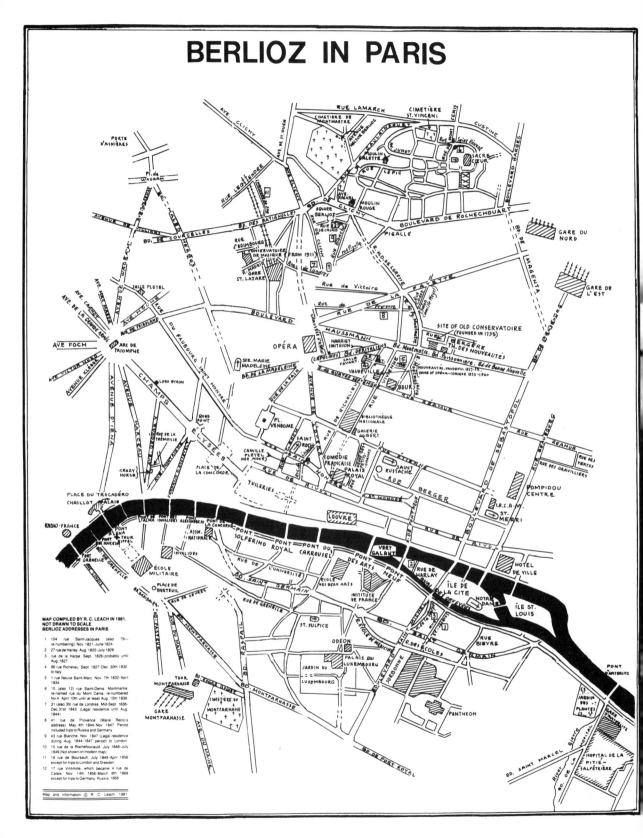

Houses in the rue Saint-Jacques, where Berlioz lodged with his cousin Alphonse Robert.

between Boulevard Poissonnière and the rue Bergère. The present day Conservatoire National Superieur de Musique has been situated at 14 rue de Madrid since 1911, the building having previously been a Jesuit College. The concert hall there is now called Salle Berlioz. The concert hall of the old Conservatoire has been preserved as it was in the time of Berlioz. It is now situated inside the Conservatoire d'Art Dramatique, rue du Conservatoire, a 'T' junction with the north side of rue Bergère, and less than a minute's walk from the site of the old Conservatoire de Musique, now occupied by the Hotel Victoria, 2 bis rue Bergère.

In October 1981 Marie Françoise Egret of the Conservatoire d'Art Dramatique arranged for the author to photograph the reconstructed

The entrance of the Schola Cantorum in the rue Saint-Jacques.

Opposite:
A map of Paris, specially compiled to show where Berlioz lived and other landmarks familiar to him.

The gardens of the Paris Conservatoire.

concert hall. It is a majestic edifice, with its red plush-seated balconies, boxes and galleries climbing to the ornate ceiling. The walls of the balconies are ornamented with faded faces and names on long murals of cracked canvas. For the interest of music historians the names on the upper gallery are as follows: Rossini, Cherubini, Mendelssohn, Méhul, Boïeldieu, Orphee, Grétry, Spontini, Donizetti, Hérold and Halévy. Names and faces round the lower balcony read: Molière, Racine, Beaumarchais, Crebillon, Eschyle, Marivaux, Regnard, Voltaire and Corneille. These, then, were the great names of Berlioz's student days, some of whom have survived the test of time while others have passed into obscurity.

On that evening in October 1981 the author attended a concert at the new Conservatoire in rue Madrid, in the concert hall named Salle Berlioz. What, one wonders, would Berlioz have thought, as critic and journalist, of the three young performers? It is virtually certain he would have been delighted. In his own day only French born or naturalized French students were admitted, so the charming young Chinese girl, Chyou-Lin, would have attracted special attention. She walked on with the gauche shyness of early youth, but her playing of Schubert, Chopin and Kabelevsky showed her artistic maturity. Would the long pink dress Chyou-Lin wore have reminded Berlioz of the pink boots of Estelle Duboeuf? He would surely have been charmed by the young girl's performance, just as he was in 1852 by young Mlle Clauss's playing in London when he wrote to the French critic Joseph-Louis d'Ortigie, who succeeded him as music critic of *Débats*, concerning the seventeen-year-old pianist—

Mlle Claus played Mendelssohn's G minor concerto with admirable purity of style, expression, finish; she had to repeat the Adagio. This child is now considered in London to be the leading lady pianist (who is also a musician) of the age . . . Don't fail to mention Mlle Clauss . . . in your next article.

Berlioz would also have enjoyed the playing of the two young men, Roel Dieltiens (cello) and Philippe Nicolai (piano accompanist). Dieltiens looked like a smart young Debussy. His first two pieces Berlioz would have understood (Beethoven and Schumann), but what would he have made of Debussy's *Sonate pour piano et violoncelle*? Would he have recognized that his fellow Conservatoire student of the future was to lead French music from Romanticism into the new world of Impressionism? Berlioz, the most honest and perceptive of critics, would indeed have recognized the major step forward in the history of music: the elusive tonal colours, the affinity with the *pointilliste* school of painters and the alliance with the poetry of Mallarmé, as well as Debussy's use of distantly related overtones.

The Salle Berlioz is smaller than the hall Berlioz himself used at the old Conservatoire. He would not have liked the new one. A high-rise building looks the same whether it is in Paris, Peru, Paraguay or Portsmouth. The same can be said of a modern concert hall. The Salle Berlioz holds about two hundred people and has a single-level wooden stage some 2ft 6in high, large enough to hold a small symphony orchestra but hardly one of Berliozian proportions. There are adjustable rectangular acoustic panels suspended over the stage, and a double microphone hanging from the hall ceiling. Berlioz would have longed for the old hall, with its ornate individuality, its boxes and galleries, its ochre, gold and amber colouring, its pictorial honouring of the great. To see the reconstructed old hall and the new hall was an education in itself.

During his early years in Paris as a student at the Conservatoire, which had been founded in 1795 by Bd. Sarrette with Cherubini on the original staff and its Director from 1822, Berlioz attended concerts at the Odéon, near the Palais de Luxembourg. The theatre was built in 1782 and given the name Théâtre Français. In 1792

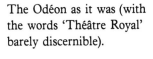

The Odéon as it was (with the words 'Théâtre Royal' barely discernible).

The Odéon today, little changed (but for the words 'Théâtre National').

Carl Maria Weber, whose *Der Freischütz* Berlioz much admired.

Republican members of the cast moved to the Comédie Française, in rue de Richelieu. The Royalists remained, but they were quickly put in prison. The name Odéon was created in 1797, but the building was burnt down in 1807. It was reconstructed, and in 1872 Bizet had a great success there with his music for Alphonse Daudet's play *L'Arlésienne*. Chalgrin, architect of the Odéon, also designed part of the Arc de Triomphe. Berlioz became very fond of the Odéon and in 1827 the theatre's chorus and orchestra came to his assistance by performing the Mass he had written in 1824 originally for choirmaster M. Masson of the church of Saint Roch. The 1827 performance, as successful as the Saint Roch one three years earlier had been disastrous, took place in the church of Saint Eustache.

Berlioz's second Paris address was a fifth floor room at 27 rue de Harlay, on the corner with the Quai des Orfèvres, on the Île de la Cité. This street, which runs right across the island, has been completely rebuilt. On the east side is the guarded, imposing Conciergerie and Palais de Justice. On the other side is the neat, pleasantly landscaped Place Dauphine. On the corner of rue de Harlay and Quai des Orfèvres there is now an elegant restaurant, Auberge du Vert Galant. The little park at the western tip of the island is still popular, and people today sit there to eat their sandwiches as Berlioz used to in the 1820s.

In 1826 he shared an apartment with Antoine Charbonnel in rue de la Harpe, on the Left Bank opposite Ile de la Cité. It is a narrow street running from Boulevard Saint-Germain to the Pont Saint-Michel which links the island to the 'mainland' of southern Paris. The buildings are very much in character, a good reflection of the Berlioz era. An inscription on the wall above number 3 reads: 'A. Cadot. arch^te—1865'.

As we have seen, it was during this period that Berlioz accepted a job in vaudeville at the old Théâtre des Nouveautés in rue Vivienne, opposite the Bourse. The theatre then was probably a brilliantly lit marquee, possibly with flaming jets of gas. The new Théâtre des Nouveautés is only a few yards from where the old Conservatoire de Musique stood in the Boulevard Poissonniere. The site of the old theatre is commemorated today by a café known as *Le Vaudeville*, and is still opposite the (new building) Bourse des Valeurs.

By 1826 Berlioz had developed strong likes and dislikes in music. Weber's *Der Freischütz*, which Berlioz admired, was slashed and re-hashed as *Robin des Bois* and put on at the Odéon in 1826. Berlioz was furious at the blatant plagiarism and distortion, especially since crowds (ignorantly, in his view) flocked to see it and handsome profits were made.

The Odéon was the National Theatre of Paris at the time. The Opéra of Berlioz's era sequentially occupied several different sites, each building in turn either destroyed by fire or removed by mid-century development of boulevards and avenues according to the plan of Baron Hausmann. These opera houses existed from 1669 until the present Opéra was completed. We know that the opera house in use in 1858 was situated in rue le Peletier. At one end is the Banque National de Paris and Boulevard Hausmann, but a walk to the other end of rue le Petelier, to Place Kossuth, reveals no evidence of the old site. There is a wall plaque above number 29 for André Honnorat (Senator des Basses Alpes) who lived there between 1890 and 1949, and the street is crossed by the rue Rossini, otherwise only the street name remains of the mid-nineteenth century Opéra of Berlioz's lifetime.

The present Paris Opéra, built by order of Napoleon III, took fourteen years to construct and was opened on 5 January 1875. It was lit by gas, and outside twenty-two wrought-iron maidens served as ornamental lamp posts. Inside, on the left of the amphitheatre entrance, is a bust of Hector Berlioz, but he of course never saw Garnier's splendid building in its completion.

The possession of a pass for the pit of the Odéon was a godsend for the impoverished music student; and it was at the Odéon, on 15 September 1827, that Berlioz experienced 'the supreme drama of my life'. He attended a performance of Shakespeare's *Romeo and Juliet* and saw for the first time Harriet Smithson, the Irish actress who was eventually to become his wife and who aroused in him a passion that led to lasting tribulations. In his *Memoirs* he asserts that the statement, 'I shall marry that woman and write my greatest symphony on that play,' was written years later by a journalist and was not his own. Nevertheless, he cannot resist saying that although he never said it, he did it. (The journalist in question was probably Charles Gruneisen of the *London Illustrated News*, c. 1848.)

In September 1827 Berlioz moved northwards from the Left Bank

One of the wrought-iron maidens flanking the entrance to the Opéra.

and took lodgings at 96 rue de Richelieu. Today number 96 is considerably smartened up; but next door, at 98, the walls are (October 1981) crusted and antiquated and no doubt very much as Berlioz would have known them. A few minutes' walk away, at number 40, there is a plaque: *Ici, s'élevait la maison où Molière né à Paris le 15 Janvier 1622, es mort le 17 Février 1673.*

Harriet Smithson was at rue Neuve Saint-Marc, which crosses rue

40 rue de Richelieu, where Molière was born.

de Richelieu with number 96 on the corner. The junction is so narrow that these Shakespearean lovers could have enacted Romeo and Juliet's balcony scene from their respective bedroom windows.

During this period, when Harriet Smithson would have nothing to do with Berlioz, Camille Moke and her shrewd mother were living very near the church of Saint Roch in the rue Honoré. Hector and Camille met as teachers at Madame Aubré's school at the Orthopaedic Institute in rue Harlay-Marais, and their passionate affair temporarily obliterated Berlioz's obsession with Harriet.

By 1830 Berlioz was familiar with the second and ninth *arrondissements*, the areas that housed the Bourse, Bibliothèque Nationale, Palais Royale, Opéra, the Conservatoire de Musique, and Salle Favart (Opéra-Comique). This area became 'home' to him in Paris. On a July day when the Revolution was at its height, he heard the crowd singing his own *Battle Hymn*, which had been published that February as *Hymn des Marseillais* for full orchestra and double choir, dedicated to Rouget de L'Isle. He accordingly went outside and marched with them as they thrust into Galerie Colbert and then surged through the arcade into rue Vivienne as well as into the arcade leading to rue Neuve-des-Petits-Champs where Berlioz, unrecognized, sang the *Marseillaise* with the triumphant mob. In August Lafayette presented Louis-Philippe to the people who crowded below the balcony of the Hotel de Ville within sight of the old Berlioz-Charbonnel ménage on the Ile de la Cité.

On his return from Italy Berlioz took up residence in his favourite Parisian district, at number 1 rue Neuve Saint-Marc, on 7 November 1832. This was his fifth address in the capital and was quite near the junction of rue Saint Marc and rue de Richelieu. He was told that Harriet had left the day before to live in rue Rivoli, and passionate memories of his old love were immediately revived. But things were not going well for Harriet. Her own company was drawing poor crowds to the Théâtre Italien in November, so poor that in the following January the players moved to a small theatre in rue Chantereine (a street that has since disappeared).

Berlioz was now inspired to declare his love in the grand manner. It was not surprising: he was a man who invariably thought and did things in the grandest of manners. So it was arranged that Harriet would be invited to occupy a box for the Berlioz concert at the Conservatoire. The programme would include the *Symphonie fantastique* together with its sequel, the monodrama *Lélio*. Surely, Berlioz reasoned, Harriet would then realize that *she* was the object of his true and only love. (The fact that the last movement of the symphony, the 'Witches' Sabbath', was written in disgust at Harriet and her earlier rejection of him does not appear to have troubled the ardent composer, even if it had occurred to him.)

The concert took place on 9 December 1832:

The symphony began and produced a tremendous effect . . . The brilliant reception, the passionate character of the work, its ardent, exalted melodies, its protestations of love, its sudden outbursts of violence, and the sensation of hearing of that size close to, could not fail to make an impression—an impression as profound as it was totally unexpected—on her nervous system and poetic imagination, and in her heart of hearts she thought, 'Ah, if he still loved me!' During the interval . . . ambiguous remarks . . . veiled allusions to the cause of this young composer's well-known trouble of the heart, began to make her suspect the truth and she heard them in growing agitation. But when Bocage, the actor who spoke the part of Lélio (that is, myself), declaimed these lines:

> Oh, if I could only find her, Juliet, the Ophelia whom my heart cries out for! If I could drink deep of the mingled joy and sadness that real love offers us, and one autumn evening on some wild heath with the north wind blowing over it, lie in her arms and sleep at last, long, sorrowful sleep!

'God!' she thought: 'Juliet—Ophelia! Am I dreaming? I can no longer doubt. It is of me he speaks. He loves me still.' From that moment, so she has often told me, she felt the room reel about her; she heard no more but sat in a dream, and at the end returned home like a sleepwalker, with no clear notion of what was happening.

The following day Berlioz obtained Miss Smithson's leave to be introduced to her. His grand plan had apparently succeeded. It did not really turn out to his advantage.

Heinrich Heine, the German poet and member of the Berlioz romantic group, who lies buried in the Cimetière de Montmartre, about thirty yards from Berlioz's own grave, describes the early Berlioz music—

He is an immense nightingale, a lark as great as an eagle . . . the music causes me to dream of fabulous empires filled with fabulous sins!

In May 1837 Heine looked back to that 1832 performance of the *Symphonie fantastique* and *Lélio* and wrote—

. . . he will remain in my memory for ever. It was in the Conservatoire at a performance of a big symphony of his, a bizarre nocturnal landscape, only occasionally lit by a sentimental white female skirt, fluttering to and fro, or by a sulphurous flash of irony. My neighbour at that performance, a garrulous young man, pointed to the composer who sat at the back of the orchestra, beating the timpani, because that's his instrument. 'Look at the front box,' said my neighbour, 'do you see that fat English woman? That's Miss Smithson; Mr. Berlioz has been desperately in love with her for three years, and we are indebted to that passion for the wild symphony we are going to hear just now . . .' Berlioz stared at her all the time, and whenever their eyes met, he hit his drum like a madman.

Opposite:
The façade of the Opéra-Comique.

A cynic might speculate on whether Harriet, in 1833, had cause to dream of fabulous empires because of Hector's music or because he was a convenient financial saviour for the Smithson entourage of

The marriage certificate of Berlioz and Harriet Smithson.

mother, sister, and bankrupt troupe of Shakespearean players. To add to her problems Harriet slipped when dismounting from a coach, on 1 March, and broke her leg. A benefit concert was arranged at Salle Favart on 2 April: Liszt and Chopin played during the entr'acte. The profits were used to settle some of Harriet's debts. Bankrupt and with her career in ruins, Harriet had every reason to welcome a helpmate. The love affair between the two was no doubt intensified by the fact that both families were against it. (Dr Berlioz had in fact selected a suitable wife for his son in La Côte Saint-André. The wedding was to take place on his return from Italy and before he returned to Paris; but Hector would have none of this marriage broking.)

Under the rules of the Prix de Rome, Berlioz was due to visit Germany. Much as he had wanted to win this prize, he seemed reluctant to abide by its rules regarding travel. Love was obviously more important: for Camille Moke's sake he had tried to delay his journey to Italy; now, in 1833, for Harriet Smithson he wanted to delay his trip into central Europe. He was in no fit mental state to study music abroad. To his confidant Humbert Ferrand he wrote that August:

I shall see Henrietta* tonight, possibly for the last time . . . It must come to an end one way or the other; I cannot go on living thus!

Towards the end of August a violent argument took place between Harriet and Berlioz, described in another letter to Ferrand—

*This was Berlioz's name for Harriet.

Despair on her part, and reproaches that I loved her no longer; tired of the struggle, I replied to that by taking poison before her eyes. Fearful shrieks from Henrietta—sublime despair—mocking laughter from me—desire to live once more on hearing her frantic avowals of love—emetic—I was ill for three days, but got over it.

Their prospects were gloomy, but poverty can act as a spur to young lovers. Harriet was heavily in debt and Hector was penniless: he had to borrow 300 francs from his friend M. Gounet to pay for the wedding. This took place in the chapel of the British Embassy on 3 October 1833. Liszt was one of the witnesses; Hiller and Heine were among those present. (The marriage certificate was later sent to Somerset House in London and is now kept in the Public Record Office, Chancery Lane.) The newlyweds honeymooned in nearby Vincennes and set up home in the familiar 1 rue Neuve Saint-Marc. A certain announcement in the London *Court Journal* was unnecessarily cruel, as well as inaccurate:

Miss Smithson was married last week, in Paris, to Delrioz [sic], a musical composer. We trust this marriage will insure the happiness of an amiable young woman, as well as secure us against her reappearance on the English boards.

The writer of that piece of spite need not have worried, for it soon became evident that Harriet's career was over. In one performance of the scene in *Hamlet* where Ophelia kneels before the veil, believing it to be her father's shroud, Harriet's recently mended leg stiffened so that she stumbled as she tried to stand up. Marie Dorval, playing at the same charity concert in the rôle of Adèle in Dumas's *Antony*, inadvertently finished her as a professional actress: Madame Dorval was given an ovation and several curtain calls, but Harriet was not called back once!

A concert conducted by Berlioz on 24 November was equally disastrous. In his worried state he forgot to bring in the second violins in the introduction of *La mort de Sardanapale*. The rules of the Théâtre Italien allowed the musicians to depart at midnight, and under cover of a Weber overture they did just that, leaving the wretched Berlioz with only a handful of players to perform the *Symphonie fantastique*. He was 'crimson with anger and mortification', and journalistic enemies were quick to intimate that it was Berlioz's music that had driven the musicians away.

However, 1833 did after all have a happy ending for Berlioz. At a concert on 22 December, which included the first performance of the overture *King Lear*, Berlioz found a most important and significant friend and supporter.

To crown my good fortune, one member of the audience stayed behind in the empty hall, a man with long hair and piercing eyes and a strange, ravaged countenance, a creature haunted by genius, a Titan among giants,

Mairie du 1er arrond.t de
Paris.

Le S.r Louis Hector Berlioz
et D.lle Henriette Constance

Smithson

ont été unis en mariage le trois
octobre, mil huit cent trente-trois.

Le Maire
Cabillot

PARIS

29864

Donné par
J. B. Weckerlin

The lane leading to the hill of Montmartre. During Berlioz's lifetime the Montmartre community considered itself separate from Paris.

whom I had never seen before . . . He stopped me in the passage and seizing my hand uttered glowing eulogies that thrilled and moved me to the depths. It was Paganini.

The friendship soon blossomed. In January 1834 Paganini visited Berlioz and asked him to write a work for solo viola and orchestra. Paganini had recently acquired a fine Stradivarius viola and was anxious to show it off to virtuoso effect, as was his custom on the violin. Unfortunately, what Berlioz originally proposed was not to Paganini's liking: it contained too many rests for the soloist. But the friendship prevailed, and Berlioz's original work was not wasted; it came out as his second 'symphony', *Harold in Italy*, for viola and orchestra, the soloist assuming the role of the introspective Harold in loosely but never specifically Byronic terms. The four movements

4 rue du Mont Cenis, Montmartre, where Berlioz lived between 1834 and 1837.

Opposite:
The French record of Berlioz's marriage, signed by the mayor of the 1ᵉʳ *arrondissement*.

77

have individual superscriptions, like the *Symphonie fantastique*, and also like that masterpiece, each makes use of an *idée fixe*.

1. Harold in the Mountains. Scenes of melancholy, happiness and joy.
2. March of the Pilgrims, singing their evening prayer.
3. Serenade of the Mountain-dweller of the Abruzzi to his mistress.
4. Orgy of brigands. Memories of past scenes.

The Italian landscape affected Berlioz every bit as much as the Byronic legend and background. He completed the symphony when he was back in Paris in 1834. Paganini never played *Harold*, though he did honour his commission and paid Berlioz for it.

In April 1834 Berlioz and Harriet moved to the 'top of the map', to 4 rue du Mont Cenis. Harriet was expecting a child. At the time the name of the hilly countryside lane dropping down the back (northern side) of Montmartre hill was called rue Saint-Denis, and the numberings of the Berlioz home there have been published as 10 (also 12) rue Saint-Denis. The couple lived there between 10 April 1834 and 15 August 1836. This was the sixth Paris address for Berlioz; a plaque on the wall reads: *Hector Berlioz. 1803-1869. Habita cette maison de 1834 à 1837. Il y composa la symphonie Harold en Italie et Benvenuto Cellini, opéra.* This plaque was erected on 11 September 1908 by the Fondation Hector Berlioz, et Société de Vieux Montmartre.

The twelfth-century church of Saint Pierre of Montmartre contains four columns from a Roman pagan temple that stood on the hilltop two thousand years ago. The 'Butte Montmartre' was then known as the 'Mountain of Mercury'. The garden to the left of the church, leading up to Berlioz's house, was known as the Garden of Calvary, a name given to the site in 1802. The Berlioz house and garden have disappeared, but some of the delicacy of the trees and shrubs can be seen today at such nearby addresses as 11B rue Giradon, or in the vegetation leading up to the Museum of old Montmartre (17 rue Saint-Vincent). The present church of Saint Pierre is the only remaining part of the great Abbey of Montmartre, founded in 1133. In the tiny cemetery are buried the sculptor Pigalle and the Debray brothers, the original owners of Moulin de la Galette.

The name when Berlioz lived there was rue Saint-Denis (the modern street of this name runs from the Seine, parallel with Boulevard Sebastopol, northwards for one mile to the Porte St Denis junction with Boulevard Saint Denis) and the name plate reads, 'rue du Mont Cenis. Ancienne rue Saint Denis'. A lover of Berlioz can, therefore, speculate on the possibility of Berlioz having influenced the choice of the new name, rue du Mont Cenis. In his *Memoirs* he writes of the journey home after his term in Italy and his re-entry into France—

Montmartre in the late 1860s, still much as Berlioz would have known it when he lived there.

Thus it was that on 12 May 1832, as I came down the Mont Cenis, I saw again in all its spring beauty the lovely valley of the Grésivaudan where the Isère winds, and where I had spent the most idyllic hours of my childhood and the first intimations of passion had come to disturb me . . . Down there in that blue haze lay my grandfather's house; it seemed to be welcoming me home . . . I felt an upsurge of pure delight—abruptly cut short by a sudden pain stabbing at my heart. I fancied I heard the distant roar of Paris.

Did Berlioz remember this when he stood on the muddy hill of Montmartre and looked down on the city of Paris? Montmartre is 350 feet above the Seine, and when Berlioz lived there it was in the country, and with its muddy lanes turned to icy hazard in the winter life must have been particularly difficult for the composer going on business trips to the city below. There was no Metro to Abbesses station, and no Funiculaire to Sacré Coeur, which was not completed until 1910.

By June 1834 Berlioz had completed *Harold in Italy* and had begun work on the opera *Benvenuto Cellini*, to a text by Wailly and Barbier. He had been able to give up some of his journalistic hack work, thanks to an advance of two thousand francs by Ernest Legouvé, to whom the overture to the opera is dedicated. Berlioz's son, Louis, was born on 14 August.

23 November saw the first performance of *Harold in Italy*, at the Conservatoire. Chrétien Urhan, principal violinist in both the Opéra and the Conservatoire orchestras, and also an outstanding viola player, was the soloist. Urhan was something of a prude: he would sit with his back to the stage so that he could not see the dancers' legs in ballet and vaudeville. He played Berlioz's solo part very badly; Girard, the conductor, also made serious mistakes, and repeated them at subsequent performances. Berlioz was saddened and resolved henceforth to conduct his music himself.

79

In September 1836 Berlioz decided he could not face another winter on the hill, so he and Harriet moved to his seventh Paris address, 31 rue de Londres, which was very much the centre of his musical activities. This remained his legal address until August 1844, and he finally relinquished his Montmartre home in 1837. One of Harriet's letters, dated 11 July 1836, is headed as from 35 rue de Londres, but one written by Berlioz on 12 December 1837 shows that the street had been renumbered for it is headed number 31, and this was the official number for the rest of his time there.

Where Berlioz and Harriet lived was opposite the north-east corner of the present Gare St Lazare. The corner buildings have disappeared and a new construction (1981) is being erected as one huge Direction Générale for the French Railways (SNCF).

Paganini, who had left for Nice immediately after expressing his disappointment with Berlioz's projected work for viola and orchestra, and already suffering from the ailment of the throat that eventually killed him, was back in Paris and was present at the concert given on 16 December 1838 at which, in Berlioz's own term, *Benvenuto Cellini* was 'slaughtered'. Paganini came away 'horrified'; fortunately he was not taken in by the hostile reaction and hastened to assure Berlioz that his music *was* superb. Berlioz recorded in his *Memoirs*:

The concert had just ended; I was worn out, lathered in perspiration and shaking all over, when Paganini, followed by his son Achille, came up to me at the orchestra door, gesticulating violently. (Paganini was suffering from cancer of the larynx and could hardly speak, so that he needed to communicate through his son.) He made a sign to the child, who stood on a chair and put his ear close to his father's mouth. Having listened carefully, the boy got down again and addressed me: 'My father bids me tell you, sir, that never in all his life has he been so affected by any concert. Your music has overwhelmed him, and it is all he can do not to go down on his knees to thank you.' At these astonishing words I made a gesture of embarrassment and incredulity; but Paganini, seizing me by the arm and hoarsely whispering with what was left of his voice, 'Yes, yes,' dragged me back onto the platform, where many of the players still lingered. There he knelt and kissed my hand. No need to describe my feelings: the facts speak for themselves.

Two days later Achille called on Berlioz and gave him twenty thousand francs, with an accompanying note from Paganini that read: 'Beethoven being dead, only Berlioz can make him live again!' For the next few days a stream of artists went to the Berlioz home to see the famous letter. As soon as it was received, Berlioz hurried to the Neothermes in rue de la Victoire, found Paganini in the billiards room, and embraced him.

Berlioz's marriage was not going well. Harriet was increasingly turning into a shrew, a harridan and an alcoholic, sour of temper and generally impossible. No doubt she deserved some sympathy; Berlioz cannot have been the easiest man to live with, but all the evidence is

Berlioz being congratulated ecstatically by Paganini after the performance of *Benvenuto Cellini*.

Marie Recio, Berlioz's mistress and later his wife.

that Harriet was never the angel her ardent suitor imagined her to be. His dreams of domestic bliss shattered, Berlioz took a mistress, the opera singer Marie Recio. Marie's home was at 41 rue de Provence, and Berlioz lived with her there until 1847. It is a pity that there is no plaque to commemorate Berlioz's stay there, if only because of his seven Paris addresses so far this is the first still to be seen in something like its original state.

Walking from the Place de la Trinité end of the rue de Londres, down rue de la Chaussée, one comes to the rue de Provence. Moving eastwards the street becomes narrower, the properties less and less modern as the house numbers decrease. There are several indications that this was the 'opera area': at number 76 the Hotel Suisse-Savoy has 'Paris Opéra' printed three times on the glass of the front door and once on the large outer-wall sign. As the Recio–Berlioz establishment is approached, the walls are cracked and blistered with age. Only at street level are the shop fronts reasonably modern. Number 41 seems to rise to the skies, its balconies protected by ornamental wrought iron railings. There are large fifteen-foot high French windows on the second floor, and on the fourth floor a long balcony links 41, 43 and 45 into one grand old building. Above, far from the narrow street below, there are seven attic windows built into the high rooftop.

At street level number 41 is now a Chinese restaurant. Happily, the operatic connections are honoured by the name: Opéra d'Aisie. Evidence that the floors above are those occupied by Berlioz and Marie Recio comes in the inscription carved into the wall of number 45, 'L'Hubert de Vandierre, 1842'. Whoever this person may have been, he was their neighbour when they lived together at number 41. Continuing down rue de Provence this authentic glimpse of Berlioz's life and times quickly disappears. From 39 to 31, the junction with rue la Fayette, the buildings are new, albeit in the style of the nineteenth century, with latticed and shuttered French windows fronted by iron railings. But there are no balconies—twentieth-century economy sees to that.

During this period the social conscience of the Western world was being increasingly alerted to the many injustices it was blindly tolerating. Laws were passed to stamp out the exploitation of children. A Factory Act of 1833 banned children under nine years old from working in factories, and there was a strong campaign to abolish slavery, not unlike the anti-apartheid demonstrations a hundred and fifty years later. There was also a degree of emancipation for women. In November 1836 Berlioz was bold enough to conduct an opera, *Esmeralda*, by Mlle Louise Bertin. This provoked a violent reaction and malicious opposition from the traditionalists. An opera by a woman! It was impossible to finish the performance: there was some applause for Quasimodo's aria, 'The Bell Song', but

41 rue de Provence, where Berlioz made his home with Marie Recio.

the chauvinistic scoffers shouted—'It's not by Louise Bertin, it's by Berlioz!'

The Bertin family were staunch supporters of Berlioz. Armand Bertin defied Cherubini and insisted that Berlioz be appointed professor of composition at the Conservatoire in 1838, but the Ministry of the Interior blocked the appointment. Berlioz's main income at this time came from journalism, and the Bertin family controlled the *Journal de Débats*—the brothers Armand and Edouard and their crippled sister Louise, the woman who had dared to write an opera. (*Esmeralda* was to a libretto after Victor Hugo's novel *Notre Dame de Paris*.)

Continuing the search for Berlioz's twelve Paris addresses, the ninth was 43 rue Blanche, where he moved in November 1847, immediately before his departure for London. There is no plaque on the wall of the present number 43 and bearing in mind Berlioz's personal reasons for disliking the name Pleyel, he might have been put out if he had known that one day in the future number 41 rue Blanche would become a piano shop, 'with four pianos in the window—all Pleyels!'

Berlioz gradually managed to free himself from vaudeville, poverty and a dependence on journalism, and could concentrate on being a composer. From the later 1830s and the 1840s come some of his finest works. Apart from the *Symphonie fantastique* and *Harold en Italie*, there was the song cycle *Les Nuits d'été* (1834-41), the opera *Benvenuto Cellini*, the Requiem (*Messe des Morts*) (1837), the *Symphonie funèbre et triomphale* (1840), *La Damnation de Faust* (1846), and a number of smaller but not necessarily insignificant works. Though it was hardly a propitious time for him on the personal plane, it was on the creative side reasonably productive.

Take *Les Nuits d'été*, a cycle of six settings of poems by Théophile Gautier. Although Berlioz does not mention him in the *Memoirs*, he and Gautier were good friends. Gautier's grave lies only some thirty yards from that of Berlioz in the Montmartre cemetery. Berlioz, who relished sentimental links, would not have failed to note that his poetical friend had the same surname as Estelle Duboeuf's grandmother at Meylan, or that Gautier lived at Villa Beaujou, 14 Avenue Byron. But the greatest tribute of composer to poet was the song cycle, which marked an important stage in Berlioz's development and in the evolution of romantic song. *Les Nuits d'été* was originally written for voice and piano, and was only orchestrated in 1856 (except for 'L'Absence', which he orchestrated for Marie Recio in 1843). It cannot therefore be truly acknowledged as the first

43 rue Blanche—and the *maison du piano* next door.

Théophile Gautier, the poet whose words Berlioz set to music in the song cycle *Les Nuits d'été*.

orchestral song cycle; that honour almost certainly belongs to Mahler's *Lieder eines fahrended gesellen*. All the same, *Les Nuits d'été* follows Beethoven's *An die ferne Geliebte* and the song cycles of Schubert, along with those of Schumann, as a landmark in the form that was characteristic of the Romantic era. If Beethoven in fact inaugurates the genius of song cycle for the German Romantics, that of Berlioz performs a similar service from the French viewpoint. In *La Presse* Gautier truly wrote: 'With Victor Hugo and Eugène Delacroix, Hector Berlioz appears to us to form the Trinity of Romantic Art.' In *Les Nuits d'été* the creative minds of Gautier and Berlioz combined most effectively.

The first of the six songs, 'Villanelle' (Country Song), has an exquisite melodic line and the chordal accompaniment is not 'hammered' out, but is delicate, tender, subtle, and full of tonal and rhythmic surprises, like the springtime it invokes. The songs of Berlioz added an operatic dimension which lifted traditional French song to new levels, just as definitely as those of Beethoven and Schubert did in Germany. When orchestrated, 'Villanelle' gained an aurally softening effect in the abrupt modulations. Berlioz employed a small orchestra of flutes, clarinets, oboe, bassoon and strings. The song moves along at a lively *allegretto*, the voice part marked *dolce* and the accompaniment *p sempre leggiero*.

The second song is the slow paced 'Le Spectre de la rose' and is an illustration of the special kind of voice required to sing Berlioz. Robert Jacobson, writing on the sleeve of Eleanor Steber's recording of Berlioz songs (CBS Classics 61430), argues that the singer of Berlioz needs 'a special quality and range associated with French opera, a soprano with a middle and lower register, or a mezzo with an expansive top range'—which sounds something like the coloratura mezzo Rossini favoured.

The third song, 'Sur les langunes', is based on a theme of gloom and despair, of a lover's lament for the dead beloved; but these tragic emotions are given strength and nobility. 'Je chant ma romance/Que le ciel entend seul./Ah! Comme elle était belle/Et comme je l'aimais!'

The fourth song, 'Absence' is usually regarded as the finest of the six. As J. H. Elliott wrote: 'The finest song in the set, without doubt, is *Absence*—a poignant and lovely thing, as individual in conception and execution as it is free from all hint of search for deliberate effect.' 'Au cimetière' has a chilly, haunting quality and a hint of the sickly sweet scent of death with the echo of the lost voices of the dead. The final song, 'L'Ile inconnue', is not quite as imposing as the others, but provides a fitting finale.

> Dites, la jeune belle!
> Où voulez-vous aller?
> La voile enfle son aile,
> La brise va souffler!

(Tell me, lovely young thing
Where do you wish to go?
The sail is on the wing,
The breeze begins to blow!)

Although it is usually female singers who nowadays address themselves to *Les Nuits d'été*, Berlioz did specify (again anticipating Mahler) that the songs could be sung by male voices, tenor for 'Villanelle', 'Absence', 'Au cimetière' and 'L'Ile inconnue', baritone for 'Sur les lagunes'. A Philips recording under Sir Colin Davis mixes male and female voices, with interesting if not entirely convincing results.

The problem of finding the right voices to sing Berlioz is worth returning to for a moment, since it was as difficult in his own day as it is in ours. Louis Alizard, a bass-baritone, was a good friend of Berlioz and became a leading exponent of his vocal music. In 1839 he sang Friar Laurence in *Roméo et Juliette*; and it was Alizard who sang the *Elégie* in Berlioz's lodgings when the young composer was sick with love for Harriet Smithson. Berlioz would not allow *Elégie* to be sung in public, and Leigh Hunt later told him that the origin of Thomas Moore's poem was the love of patriot Robert Emmet for Sarah Curran. A certain bass singer, M. Serda, made a mess of the part of the Cardinal in *Benvenuto Cellini*, so Alizard took his place and sang the role at sight.

Gilbert Duprez was another good friend of Berlioz who sang in *Benvenuto Cellini*. He made his debut at the Odéon in 1825 and gave the first performance of 'Absence' in 1843. Duprez dominated the Paris opera during the decade 1837–47, displacing Adolphe Nourrit, who in 1830 at the height of his own popularity sang, tricolour in hand, the *Marseillaise* at the reopening of the Opéra. The knowledge that Duprez had become a better singer was too much for Nourrit, and he committed suicide in 1839. Duprez himself did not last all that long in the top flight: Berlioz replaced him in *Benvenuto Cellini*, but Duprez did not take his life—instead, he went into teaching. A tenor who sang Faust in the first performance of *La Damnation de Faust* in 1846, and took the solo part in the Requiem in the same year, was Gustave-Hippolyte Roger, who also suggested to Berlioz that he should orchestrate Schubert's *Erlkönig*. Joseph Staudigl, a German bass popular in London, sang in *Faust* and as Friar Laurence in *Roméo et Juliette*. He died in a lunatic asylum, as did the impresario Louis-Antoine Jullien, who was also active in London.

The women singers of Berlioz were no less a problem, beginning with his own mistress, Marie Recio. In a letter to August Morel, Berlioz wrote:

Pity me, my dear Morel. Marie insisted upon singing at Mannheim, Stuttgart and Hechingen. On the first two occasions it was endurable—but the last!—and the bare idea of another singer disgusts her . . .

According to M. Rolland, Marie Recio was 'a mediocre singer with a mania for singing'. In 1843 Mendelssohn heard her sing 'Absence', and when asked what he thought of the performance paused, and then congratulated Berlioz on the double bass entry. What he thought of the singer is not revealed. Then there was Rosina Stoltz, who had the same power over the Opéra director Pillet as Marie Recio had over Berlioz. Thus, in 1841, Rosina was allowed to transpose down her part of Agathe in Weber's *Der Freischütz*. When she sang Ascanio in *Benvenuto Cellini*, in 1838–9, Berlioz would not allow such liberties. She had frequent clashes with Berlioz (including, it is believed, that passionate interlude in Russia) and she was furious when she did not get the part of Dido in *Les Troyens à Carthage*.

If, despite the new 'operatic dimension' of the songs, *Les Nuits d'été* is a leading example of the lyrical and refined side of Berlioz's art, the Requiem, or *Messe des morts*, represents the other, equally characteristic side. It was a leading example of the huge 'architectural works' that exploit his taste for the gigantic and set him firmly down in the nineteenth century. These works require enormous forces (the Requiem includes four brass bands in addition to vast choruses and orchestra), but like Mahler after him Berlioz was a master at producing his most memorable effects by deploying his huge forces piecemeal, as it were, and by drawing from them contrasting tonal combinations of comparatively few instruments playing together, often in unusual registers. Magniloquent and rhetorical he could certainly be, as much so as Liszt or Wagner; but he also had a most fastidious mind and ear and could compose music of the utmost delicacy and refinement. He was in this respect, as in many others, very French.

The Requiem, commissioned by the French government to honour those who had fallen in the 1830 Revolution, was one of Berlioz's first and major successes. He was obliged to work hard to obtain the commission. There was a reshuffle in the cabinet and Rossini became favourite for the task. Cherubini was also furious that his Mass was not being used. Berlioz overcame all the intrigues and the original commission was honoured—but Haberneck was in charge of State musical occasions, so he had to conduct. The first performance took place at the Invalides, for which the work was designed in the first place. Berlioz, not trusting his conductor, stood close by. And it was as well. After the Dies Irae came four strong beats to bring in the Tuba mirum. Haberneck stopped conducting and took a pinch of snuff. Berlioz leapt to the podium and conducted the absolutely essential four bars of the new tempo, and so saved the situation. Ever since, the question 'Was it deliberate?' has been asked. It has not been satisfactorily answered. What Liszt called 'this prodigious and indeed sublime work' was saved from disaster by its composer's prompt action, an action based on his suspicions from the outset. Charles Hallé, who was present at the Invalides, was inclined to put it down to incompetence. Either way, Berlioz was proved right.

After the success of the Requiem Berlioz had trouble obtaining his fee, out of which he had to pay the participants (including 300 francs to Haberneck!). He was told that all the money was gone, but that the government was considering awarding him the cross of the Légion d'honneur.

'Damn your cross,' was his immediate response. 'Give me my money!' He got it.

Another 'architectural' work, the *Symphonie funèbre et triomphale*, also came into being as a result of the Revolution of July 1830. It was commissioned by the Minister of the Interior in 1840 to celebrate the tenth anniversary of that occasion, and the re-interment of the bodies of the fallen in the Revolution beneath the column on the Place de Bastille. In its original form it was by design outdoor music, again scored for huge forces, in this case a vast array of wind and brass and percussion, in fact an engorged military band,* and large choir. The first movement, a long funeral march, was to be played as the cortège proceeded to the Place, the second is a funeral oration, with impressive sections for solo trombone which must surely have been noted later by both Mahler and Sibelius, and the third a joyously celebratory 'Apotheosis' in which the choir finally takes part.

Berlioz soon discovered the drawbacks of outdoor music, even with his enormous forces, so he added strings and turned it effectively into a concert hall work. There was a further open-air production, in 1846, using 1800 performers, but it was still not satisfactory and only confirmed Berlioz's view that the concert hall was its proper place. The string section as added was some eighty strong and is marked *ad libitum*. It is an extraordinary composition in many ways, though as with the Requiem the huge forces do not necessarily mean a huge noise. Some of the material was taken over from the unfinished opera *Les francs juges*.

Despite a fair level of productivity and the success of the Requiem, everyday life for Berlioz remained a constant irritant, especially since his return from Italy and his marriage to Harriet. 'On my return from Italy,' he wrote in 1855, 'began my Thirty Years' War against routineers, the professors, and the deaf . . .' With poor Harriet in her present sorry state he might have added, 'and with the lame'!

How quickly Harriet's star had set. As recently as 3 March 1828 she had been the toast of Paris, only ten years after her debut in London. At the Paris benefit concert in 1828, given for her at the Opéra, it is reported that a thousand people were turned away. The King gave her a purse full of gold and the Duchesse de Berry a

*The score also contains parts for instruments rare in France at the time, such as double bassoon and bass trombone.

87

valuable vase. Five years later Berlioz was trying unsuccessfully to persuade such dramatists as Victor Hugo, Alfred de Vigny (Berlioz misspelt it 'Devigny') and George Sand to write her a new play, but no one would cooperate. After her marriage Harriet aged quickly, became a nagging wife, and took to drink.

Berlioz met Marie Recio in either 1841 or 1842, and she quickly became his mistress. After Harriet's death in 1854 he married Marie, but more out of a sense of honour than of real love. She was the daughter of a French captain and a Spanish woman named Sotera Vilas. Although she was a singer, Berlioz did not at all like the shrill tone of her voice. Her hold over him was entirely physical. She died at the age of forty-eight. Her mother remained devoted to Berlioz, who appears to have retained a genuine affection for her even though her Spanish-inflected French offended his sensitive ear.

Despite his many subsequent changes of home in Paris, Berlioz always kept in touch with Harriet. Both he and their son (on leave from Cherbourg at the time) were with her on the day she died, 3 March 1854. Berlioz's grief was genuine and mixed with pity for Harriet's misfortunes—her broken heart, her vanished beauty, her

19 rue de Boursault, where Berlioz moved in 1849.

ruined health and loss of speech and movement. For the last four years of her life she was paralysed.

The 1850s began on a sad note for Berlioz. His elder sister Nanci died of breast cancer. Writing of this in the *Memoirs* Berlioz makes his views on euthanasia abundantly clear: it is a problem as difficult today as it was during the early nineteenth century:

My beloved Adèle, my other sister, who went to Grenoble to nurse her [Nanci] . . . nearly died herself from exhaustion and the horror of watching this long martyrdom.

Yet no doctor dared have the humanity to end it once and for all with a little chloroform. They do it so as to spare patients the pain of an operation which lasts a few seconds, but they will not consider using it to save them six months of torture, when it is absolutely certain that no remedy, not even time, will cure the disease, and death is clearly the only remaining boon, the sole source of happiness.

The law, however, is against it, and the doctrines of religion are no less rigidly opposed . . .

How meaningless are all these questions of fate, free will, the existence of God, and the rest of it: an endless maze in which man's baffled understanding wanders helplessly lost.

In 1848 Berlioz had returned to a devastated Paris, to find a new government (not kindly disposed towards the composer). Like the artists returning to Paris in the late 1940s, he had to spend the later 1840s rebuilding his artistic life in the capital. He had been in London (he returned there in 1851), but in Paris his career was disorganized by the inevitable street fighting and the collapse of the 1848 Revolution.

For just one year, between July 1848 and July 1849, Berlioz lived at 15 rue de la Rochefaucauld, a name which no longer appears on the street map of Paris. In the summer of 1849 he moved to 19 rue de Boursault, his eleventh Paris address and near the railway which now runs from Gare Saint-Lazare. He used this address until April 1856, except for his journeys abroad.

The small cemetery in Montmartre where Harriet was buried.

4 rue de Calais, where Berlioz lived from 1856 until his death in 1869.

The death of Harriet revealed anew to Berlioz the full stature of Shakespeare. The English bard would have understood, did understand, how artists can love and hurt each other. 'Shakespeare! Shakespeare!' he exclaims in the *Memoirs* under the twin stresses of the deaths, though four years apart, of his sister and his wife.

I feel as if he alone of all men who ever lived can understand me . . . Shakespeare! You were a man. You, if you still exist, must be a refuge for the wretched. It is you that are our father, our father in heaven, if there is a heaven. God standing aloof in his infinite unconcern is revolting and absurd. Thou alone for the soul of artists are the living and loving God.

Berlioz had to attend alone to the final duties on his dead wife's behalf. He had to take a cab to the other side of Paris to contact the Protestant pastor, and *en route* he drove past the Odéon, where he had first fallen in love with Harriet. That night he had witnessed the whole audience weep at the sight of his 'Ophelia' and he recalled again the magnitude of her triumph before the intellectual but fickle élite of Paris. Now she was gone, and almost forgotten. Twenty-five years ago all Paris would have attended her funeral; but that was all in the past, and she was buried in a small cemetery in Montmartre with but two or three friends to support Berlioz at the ceremony. She died dreaming of glories that come so swiftly, and so swiftly fade. Liszt, the understanding friend, wrote to Berlioz from Weimar: 'She inspired you, you loved her and sang of her; her task was done.'

A month after Harriet's death Berlioz wrote from Brunswick to his favourite uncle, Felix Marmion, expressing something of his feelings:

Poor Harriet had such a deep understanding of the world of poetry! She had an intuition of things she had never learnt. Besides, she revealed Shakespeare to me, and God knows what an influence that revelation has had, and will continue to have, upon my career . . . Hence the impossibility . . . of my ever forgetting her.

Henri-Auguste Barbier, co-librettist with Leon de Wailly of *Benvenuto Cellini*, appreciated that Berlioz took Shakespeare's texts as a kind of lay scripture. After a funeral he would return home and read Shakespeare. Barbier recalls one such occasion: 'We went upstairs and when settled, he began reading the scene from *Hamlet* at Ophelia's tomb. His emotion was intense and two streams of tears fell from his eyes.' On another occasion, on 17 October 1864, Berlioz was at Château de la Muette in the Passy district of Paris where the Érard family and Spontini's widow lived. They listened enraptured as Berlioz read extracts from *Othello*.

Berlioz worked a good deal abroad during the middle years of the nineteenth century, especially in London. He found appreciation for his work far greater in other countries than in his own. In return he had the highest regard for Virgil, and for Shakespeare and Byron. On

Commemorative plaque on the wall of 4 rue de Calais.

his return from London in April 1856 he settled in his final home, at 17 rue Vintimille which, that November, became 4 rue de Calais. Here he lived until he died. There is a commemorative plaque which reads: *Dans cette maison est mort le 8 Mars 1869 Hector Berlioz, compositeur de musique; né a La Côte S'André, le 11 Decembre 1803.*

6 Berlioz in London and elsewhere

Surrounded by the pettiness of the Parisian musical world, Berlioz was shabbily treated by France. Composers were expected to be orthodox in style and character, and Hector was certainly not that. He was a fundamentally unhappy person, ambitious, generous, honest, extraordinarily clear sighted and level headed, a man of strong musical likes and dislikes, and one capable of giving lucid reasons for his tastes. But his voice was very much that of 'one crying in the wilderness', recalling St Matthew's, 'A prophet is not without honour, save in his own country.' The few shreds of comfort and musical support came mostly from people who were not French. The Paris-based Hungarian Franz Liszt wrote to Ferdinand Denis in September 1838: 'I hear this evening that Berlioz's opera *Benvenuto Cellini* was not a success. Our poor friend! Fate treats him harshly! . . . Berlioz is and remains the most vigorous musical brain in France . . .' Italian-born Niccolò Paganini was Berlioz's supporter when *Benvenuto Cellini* was 'slaughtered', and bravely spoke out: '. . . if I were director of the Opéra I would immediately commission that young man to write three more operas, pay him for them in advance, and get a very good bargain out of it.' Berlin-born Giacomo Meyerbeer and the King of Prussia were two devoted supporters of *La Damnation de Faust*, the Berlioz cantata that Paris so contemptuously cast aside.

Between 1841 and 1843 Berlioz made visits to Germany and was enthusiastically received by 'excellent German artists who welcomed me so courteously'. In Leipzig he met again his companion from the Rome days, Felix Mendelssohn, and they ceremoniously exchanged batons. Marie Recio travelled with him as often as she could, but as she would insist on singing Berlioz was not always happy about her presence. When she accompanied him on another German trip in 1844/45 she did not sing and easier peace reigned between them.

When he came to the end of his first long and arduous tour of Germany, he hoped that its success would influence the authorities, in particular Léon Pillet, the director of the Opéra, to appoint him conductor at the Opéra. Unfortunately Berlioz had upset Rosina Stoltz, Pillet's mistress, so he was not appointed. Intrigue once again thwarted his legitimate ambitions.

He returned to Paris in May 1846 and decided to put on a concert of his own version of the Faust legend as the special attraction. It was not a wise move. The copying of parts was expensive, the fee of 1600 francs for the hire of the Opéra-Comique was exorbitant, and the critics complained that his Faust was unlike that of Goethe, conveniently ignoring the fact that the same could be said of Marlowe's play or Spontini's opera. An accountant could have pointed out to Berlioz that a loss was inevitable, especially as the hall was not available for an evening so it meant a midday concert. But Berlioz relied on his new-found prestige following his German successes; he also remembered that he had encountered the same gigantic expenses in putting on his *Roméo et Juliette* symphony but had still come away with a small profit. So he went ahead.

It was November, and snowing; the hall was half-empty, and it was a financial calamity for poor Berlioz. 'I was ruined. I owed a considerable sum of money which I had not got . . . I thought I saw a way out of my entanglement, I would go to Russia.' For once, it was an excellent decision. He had partly prepared the way by dedicating, in 1845, his *Symphonie fantastique* to Tsar Nicholas I. Another good omen was the generosity of a number of his friends who lent or gave him money to help him on his journey. This tour turned out to be an even greater triumph than his German, Austrian and Belgian ones had been. It restored his faith in himself and his fortunes.

On the way home from Russia, he gave a successful concert of *Faust* in Berlin in June 1847, and received an ovation that offset the Paris failure. At first the members of the orchestra had been hostile, apparently because of something Berlioz had said or written, but they were true musicians and readily acclaimed the score as a masterpiece.

He arrived back in France in September 1846. He first visited La Côte Saint-André, where he and his young son Louis enjoyed the company at the Berlioz family home. This short but happy holiday over, Berlioz returned to the cut and thrust of his life in Paris. Pillet was on the point of giving up the directorship of the Opéra. Nestor Roqueplan and Charles-Edmond Duponchel, who had been director before Pillet, wanted to share the directorship jointly. They approached Berlioz to support them. Would he see that favourable comments appeared in the *Journal des Débats*? And would he persuade Armand Bertin to intercede for them with the Minister of the Interior, who was hostile? They made promises—

If we are appointed, we will offer you an important position at the Opéra. We will make you general musical director, with the post of principal conductor thrown in . . . we will divide that post equally between you and M. Girard (the present conductor). Leave it to us; everything will be arranged to your satisfaction.

Despite Bertin's reluctance because of his suspicion of the two gentlemen, he agreed to speak to the Minister, and Roqueplan and Duponchel were duly appointed—and immediately forgot all about their promises to Berlioz. They began to snub him; there was no post available for him. Girard* refused to share the conducting, and in addition maintained Haberneck's policy of excluding Berlioz's music both at the Conservatoire and at the Opéra. The two directors continued to insult Berlioz. When he did manage to corner them, after endless evasions, they spoke of allowing him to take over the chorus, then, in a deliberately offensive afterthought, added: 'But, of course, you can't play the piano.' On top of these humiliations they reminded Berlioz, who had been working on a grand opera entitled *La nonne sanglante*† which Pillet had commissioned, that there was a ministerial regulation prohibiting artists employed at the Opéra from having their works performed in it, so if Berlioz were to be given a position, he would not be able to write operas. The implications were obvious. All former promises and undertakings were being ignored— they were doing everything they could to get rid of him. He was incensed by such colossal ingratitude and their obvious contempt for his music. But he kept his temper, and when an offer came from London for him to conduct the Grand English Opera, he immediately packed his bags. Words from Byron's *Childe Harold's Pilgrimage* might have fitted that Berliozian crossing of the Channel which, starting from Paris and aiming for London, took some sixteen hours in those days, crossing to Folkestone by steam packet:

> Adieu, adieu! my native shore
> Fades o'er the waters blue.

The offer from London had come from Louis Antione Jullien, who was born in the Basses-Alpes in 1812, not far from Berlioz's home territory in south-eastern France. He had been unsuccessful as a musician in Paris, but moved to London in or about 1840. He was an effervescent extrovert whose crazy enthusiasm was infectious and was passed on to all those around him. He lived, worked, dreamed and planned in the grand manner. He believed his mission was to bring good music to the masses and he was one of the first to put on low-priced popular concerts with a judicious blend of dance music and extracts from the classics. He was thus in many ways a forerunner of Newman and Henry Wood, the founders of the Promenade Concerts that have lasted to this day, albeit in a somewhat different form. Jullien was part serious musician, part showman. He would conduct Beethoven's music with a jewelled baton and clean gloves served to him on a silver salver. He toyed with the sensational. At one time he considered setting the Lord's Prayer to music so that all would be able to see in print: 'Words by Jesus Christ, Music by Antoine Jullien.' He was satisfied with nothing less than the best

*Narcisse Girard: he died in 1860 while conducting a performance of Meyerbeer's *Les Huguenots*.
†This opera remained unfinished.

94

The Theatre Royal, Drury Lane, in the early nineteenth century.

talent available, and when he contemplated an opera season at Drury Lane it was on the most lavish scale.

The theatrical background in the London Berlioz went to was crowded and competitive. Drury Lane had opened as the Theatre Royal, Brydges Street, in 1663 but soon adopted the more fashionable address. In 1732 Covent Garden Theatre opened and was in continual rivalry with Drury Lane. Grimaldi, said to be the greatest clown of all time, made his name at Drury Lane. The theatre was burnt down in 1809, but was then rebuilt. (During World War II it was damaged in air raids, and *The Times* of 16 November 1940 claimed that it was the oldest theatre in the world still in use.)

As if two theatre buildings close to each other were not enough, there was a third, the Lyceum, or, as it was known in the early days, the English Opera. It was opened in 1801 by Mr Lonsdale, former stage manager of Sadler's Wells, but inevitably lacked support and remained closed for several years. It did not become a regular theatre until 1809 when the company of Drury Lane obtained permission to use it until their own burnt-out building had been restored. In 1815 the Lyceum was granted a 99-year lease from the Marquess of Exeter. Michael Balfe, a Drury Lane violinist turned composer, undertook the management of the Lyceum in 1841, with plans to create a national opera after the Continental form, performing works worthy to stand beside the productions of Italy and Germany. Queen

95

The Lyceum, opened in
1801 as the English Opera.

Victoria headed the list of subscribers, and by 1843 the Lyceum was
the nearest approach to legitimate theatre in England. Charles Dillon
took over the management in 1856, and raised the price of the stalls
from five to six shillings. It was sold to the LCC in 1939 and became
a postwar dance hall. Gielgud's *Hamlet* was the last theatre
performance there.

To add to the congestion of theatres, opera houses and concert
halls in this area near the Strand was the Exeter Hall, where Berlioz
was to give successful concerts, and where the Strand Palace Hotel
now stands. With this jostling competition in London's theatreland,
Jullien was impossibly generous in the terms of the contract he
offered Berlioz.

Exeter Hall in the Strand, where Berlioz conducted a number of successful concerts.

The details of the contract were complex: £400 plus expenses between 1 December 1847 and 1 March 1848, with the stipulation that Berlioz must not conduct any other orchestra in England without permission; in addition, he had to give no fewer than four concerts within one month for a further £400, and compose an opera for Drury Lane before October 1848. It has been calculated that this contract was worth 40,000 francs a year, a veritable fortune in those days. The imagination of Berlioz was fired and he formed ambitious plans in his mind covering a period of six years. He significantly arrived in England on Fireworks Night, 5 November 1847, and he wrote to his friends in France and Russia that France was musically

Berlioz lived happily in this house in Harley Street during his visit to London in 1847–8.

stupid but England offered him the scope he had always longed for. He lived in a fine apartment at 76 Harley Street; Marie had been left behind in Paris, and life was wonderful. (Unfortunately, the unsuspecting J. W. Davison, music critic of *The Times*, was in Paris at the time and Marie persuaded him to escort her to London in December 1847.)

The opera season at Drury Lane opened on 6 December with Donizetti's *Lucia di Lammermoor*, Berlioz conducting. It was a success from the musical point of view, but Jullien had been so lavish that the production lost money. Other operas followed: Mozart's *Figaro*, Donizetti's *Linda di Chamounix* and Balfe's *Maid of Honour*;

Richard Wagner, whom Berlioz met in London in 1855.

but the financial situation became more and more desperate. For Berlioz the honeymoon period with the flamboyant Jullien was soon over. In a letter to August Morel dated 14 January 1848, he complained that he was being worked like a mill-horse, rehearsing every day from 12 to 4 and conducting nightly from 7 till 10. London club life bored him, so he preferred to spend what spare time he had with a small circle of friends, one of whom was Julius Benedict, the German-born naturalized English composer and conductor who in his youth had studied with Hummel and Weber, and who now lived at 2 Manchester Square, just behind the present Trinity College of Music. The side of the road linking Trinity College to Manchester Square is Hinde Street, and at number 8 lived the violinist Prosper Sainton. It was also at this address that Berlioz met Wagner in 1855, an occasion that brought forth from the egocentric Wagner, always highly conscious of his own suffering, the remark that, 'on the whole I think I am happier than Berlioz'. That anyone should have appeared to Wagner as unhappier than himself is a kind of achievement in itself. Other London friends and acquaintances included Thackeray, Adelaide Proctor (who wrote the words of *The Lost Chord*), Charles Dickens, Georgina Hogarth, Adolfe Ganz, Charles Hallé, and many others.

Four doors away from Berlioz's London address, at 19 (previously 80) Harley Street was the home of a Mme Dulcken, who gave musical parties in her apartment and thus brightened many a gloomy English Sunday afternoon of the kind that had so depressed Richard

George Cruikshank's view of life in Drury Lane.

The Princess's Theatre in Oxford Street.

Wagner. Berlioz was a frequent visitor. At one such gathering he heard a band in the street playing the *Marseillaise* with a phrase in the minor key that should have been major. He remarked on this to a guest, William Kuhe, and it was noted. Mme Dulcken herself was a good pianist and an enthusiastic musical organizer. She arranged an annual concert at Covent Garden, and Berlioz conducted his *Hungarian (Rakoczy) March*; in return she played at one of his concerts at the Hanover Square Rooms. Mme Dulcken played hostess to most of the leading musical personalities who visited London.

Berlioz was aware that because Mendelssohn had just died in Leipzig, on 4 November 1847, the very day Berlioz had left Paris for London, there was scope for someone to win the hearts of the English as Mendelssohn had done through the concerts he regularly conducted in the British Isles. This situation encouraged Berlioz to arrange concerts, and he threw himself energetically into the complicated ramifications of concert promotion. He listened patiently to Jullien's sad news of finances and, along with other artists, agreed to his salary being reduced by a third. This was in fact only a paper agreement, because the artists had not received any money anyway. The workmen had been paid, but that was so that the theatre could remain open.

1848 began badly for Berlioz; the weather, work and worry combining to give him a severe attack of bronchitis. In a letter dated 28 January, he claimed that his illness was brought on by 'anger, disgust and grief'. What encouraged him to continue was the genuine love of music which the British public displayed. On the other hand, the lax behaviour of the English musicians infuriated the businesslike French conductor. Rehearsals were a shambles, something which Berlioz was not unaccustomed to in his own country. But there was a

100

difference: from the chaos of an English rehearsal, a concert performance was expected in record time. At first Berlioz was fascinated and happily claimed that it was the English who had brought the art of speeded-up rehearsing to a pitch unknown to other nations. In Paris it would take ten months to learn and stage an opera; in London, ten days. There was a philosophic malaise that, whatever happened at rehearsals, the show must go on because it had been advertised and seats sold. There seemed to be frenetic races to beat records: '*We* put on our opera after only two weeks' rehearsal!'—'We put *ours* on after only ten days' rehearsal!'

Berlioz was soon horrified by all this wild hurry when he saw the results. He became especially infuriated at the illogicality of the belief that this talent for speed in preparation was a virtue worthy of the highest praise. There was an unshakeable belief that everything would be all right on the night. If the orchestra turned up and there were no band parts available, a bland, 'It's all right, we still have six days!' was all the help the dumbstruck Berlioz could expect.

London audiences, like those in European countries other than France, began to appreciate the majestic talent of Berlioz. Prior to his arrival in London in person, introductions to his music had not been propitious. On 30 March 1840 Henry Forbes gave *Les francs juges* overture at the Harmonica Society, in a hall adjoining Her Majesty's Theatre. It was not well received. The following year, Charles Lucas conducted *Benvenuto Cellini* at a Philharmonic Concert, and it was hissed. The omens, therefore, were hardly good for Berlioz in 1848, but his own persistence and the fair-mindedness of English audiences prevailed and he was shown the respect he truly deserved.

Queen Victoria and Prince Albert were very fond of music, and this encouraged a new phase in the public interest in orchestral music, with the introduction of promenade concerts based on the French style. In the winter of 1840 there were three series running—at Drury Lane, the Lyceum, and the Princess's Theatre. The Princess's was in Oxford Street, on the site of the present Waring and Gillow store. It was built in 1839 on land that had been the 'Royal Bazaar'. It opened in 1840 and was second only to Drury Lane as the home of melodrama. Its owner, who answered to the name 'Hamlet' and was a silversmith by trade, intended to use it as an opera house, but it fulfilled this function only for short periods, and its fortunes went from bad to worse. Such melodramatic productions as *Drink*, *After Dark* and *The Fatal Wedding* restored matters for a time and actually made the names of such stars as Ellen Terry, Charles Keen (who took over the management in 1850) and Wilson Barrett. Operas produced at the Princess's included Bellini's *La Sonnambula*. The production of operas was under the direction of a Mr Maddox. Berlioz would pass this theatre on his daily walk from Harley Street to Drury Lane.

If only there had been *one* theatre producing opera, *one* opera company, and *one* musical director—Hector Berlioz—opera in England in the mid-nineteenth century might well have rivalled the best in Italy or Germany. The love of good music was inherent in the English (despite their inability to produce any composers of real stature), and there was royal patronage from Victoria and Albert. But Antoine Jullien was losing his wits and Berlioz could see little hope of establishing an English national opera on the scale he envisaged. And so, his bronchitis relieved, he threw himself into arrangements for his first London concert.

This took place on 7 February 1848, and the programme included *Harold en Italie, Carnaval Romain, Benvenuto Cellini* (overture), fragments of *Faust* and the Requiem. This gigantic concert lasted for four hours. The *Faust* music electrified the audience, the 'Hungarian March' was encored, and so was 'Dance of the Sylphs'. The press reports were very good. Berlioz was fêted at the anniversary dinner given by the Royal Society of Musicians, and Hogarth, Charles Dickens's father-in-law, praised him in the *Daily News*. There was no doubt about his success as a composer, but it still brought him insufficient material reward for him to continue thinking in terms of a six-year stay in London. Indeed, in May 1848 he was forced to move out of Harley Street to more modest quarters in Osnaburgh Street, at the Regents Park end of Regent Street. Number 26 (and number 20) have been completely demolished and a new block of flats now stands on the site. By coincidence, number 26 Osnaburgh Street had previously been used by Berlioz's friend the poet Heinrich Heine when he was in exile in 1827.

On 21 March 1848 Berlioz began work on his *Memoirs*. He gave two reasons for embarking on this task: first, he wished to correct the many errors and inaccuracies which were already circulating about him; second, to disclose the difficulties confronting those who wanted to be composers. He despaired for the art of music in Europe because the military juggernaut of republicanism was on the move. In the comparative security of England Berlioz felt free to write as an observer, as he saw in the Preface: '. . . flocks of frightened artists come hurrying from all points to seek refuge, as sea-birds fly landwards before great storms. Will the British capital be able to maintain so many exiles? . . . England, since I have lived here, has treated me most warmly and hospitably . . . Who knows what will have become of me in a few months—I have no sure means of support for myself and my dependants.'

The mind of Berlioz never ceased its inquisitive foraging. While he was at 26 Osnaburgh Street he continued the study of the harmonic resonances of clocks which he had begun in Germany. At Mannheim he had noted that a nearby clock had a resonance of a minor third. Observations in other German towns convinced him of the inaccurate conclusions reached by certain eminent theorists. Berlioz now had the satisfaction of finding a new interval in the clock of Holy Trinity round the corner. It was a major third.

Although the Jullien enterprises were of no financial benefit to him, Berlioz knew that the prospects for making money in London were better than in revolution-torn Paris.

Yet love of country dies hard, and despite his liking for English audiences and his despair at the rejection of himself and his works by the Parisians, he was heart and soul a Frenchman. A letter dated 16 May 1848 reads: '. . . once I am at the end of my resources, there will be nothing for me to do but go and sit in the gutter and die of hunger like a lost dog, or blow out my brains . . . But one may as well do it in Paris as here.' He had been in England little over six months, and already his thoughts were turning homewards. His ambition to give, and to attend, concerts in London remained alive. He saw the crowds at the stage door of Her Majesty's Theatre waiting to catch a glimpse of Jenny Lind, and he went to one of the concerts given by the 'Swedish Nightingale'. He also heard Beethoven's *Fidelio* at Her Majesty's. At the corner of Hanover Street in Hanover Square were the Queen's Concert Rooms; but the local residents would not tolerate too much noise, so when on 29 June a concert there included the *Rakoczy March* it had to be given without drums or cymbals.

Paris was in turmoil following the fall of King Louis-Philippe, and one of the artists to seek refuge in London was Berlioz's close friend Charles Hallé. The two met at Harley Street and Hallé found lodgings at 28 Maddox Street. Berlioz greatly admired Hallé, and the admiration was mutual. Hallé wrote a graphic description of Berlioz the conductor, '. . . and what a picture he was at the head of his orchestra, with eagle face, his bushy hair, his air of command, and glowing with enthusiasm. He was the most perfect conductor I ever set eyes on.' And Berlioz called Hallé a model pianist and a musician '*sans peur et sans reproche*'.

Yet despite all this and his understandable desire to establish himself in England, Berlioz still felt compelled to return to France. When he finally made the decision to leave, in July 1848, the London *Musical Times* wrote: 'Hector Berlioz has left England. We feel that a great and original mind has gone from among us.'

He arrived back to find the Parisians burying their dead. It seemed that whenever Berlioz returned to Paris he was met by bad news. As if the havoc caused by the Revolution was not enough (even the 'Spirit of Liberty' on top of the Bastille column had a bullet through her body), he received news that his father had died, ten years after his mother. He went to La Côte Saint-André, but arrived too late for the funeral. His father had finally confessed that he wanted to hear and understand Hector's music, especially the Requiem, which included the Dies Irae that France had reluctantly accepted as a masterpiece. Father and son had forgotten their early battles over music as a career, and the two men had grown very close. Now Dr Berlioz would never hear and understand his son's music.

Death was commonplace that year. His friend Augustin de Pons chose 1848 to commit suicide. Berlioz hated the bestiality of the 1848 Revolution. All Europe seemed to have descended to its lowest level. Art was dead. Heroes and brave men were dead, but not killed in a clean straightforward manner, by bullet or guillotine, but horribly and slowly. Germany was no better than France. German peasants, counterparts of the French revolutionaries, killed Prince Lichnowsky in Frankfurt on 18 September. The newspaper account of the killing sickened Berlioz:

They stabbed him repeatedly with knives, hacked at him with scythes, tore his arms and legs to shreds, shot him in more than twenty places but in such a way as *not to kill him*, stripped him and left him dying at the foot of a wall. He lived for five hours.

Berlioz remembered the prince in his Paris days, and again on the return from Russia when the two met in Berlin. To Berlioz Lichnowsky was a noble, clever, generous and brave man. His murderers were 'Vile human scum, a thousand times more bestial and brainless in [your] fatuous revolutionary antics than the baboons and orangutangs of Borneo!' He declared that he must rush out into the fresh air and clear his mind of the horror by working hard at his compositions.

He left La Côte Saint-André as soon as he had played his part in settling his father's estate. Before returning to Paris Berlioz made a sentimental journey to Grenoble and the house of his grandfather at Meylan. It was but a step or two to the old home of Madame Gautier where Estelle Duboeuf had spent holidays and Berlioz had secretly worshipped her. She had married Casimir Fornier, a lawyer, but he had died in 1845. Who knows what thoughts passed through the mind of Berlioz in 1848? In his *Memoirs* he wrote—

Estelle must have come here. Perhaps I stand in the very same portion of air where her enchanting form once stood . . . I breathe the blue air that she breathed . . . I throw myself on my knees and cry, 'Estelle! Estelle!' to the valley and the hills and the sky . . . an access of loneliness, intense, overwhelming, indescribable. Bleed, my heart! bleed! only, leave me the power to suffer . . .

Back in Paris the loneliness was just as intense. Berlioz arrived in September to find the theatres shut, artists ruined and teachers of music unemployed. It seemed as though all doors were closed to him. He threw himself into the task of composing a *Te Deum*. In 1849 he was again writing criticisms for the *Journal des Débats* and the *Gazette Musicale*. Musical activities in Paris were still very much at a standstill, but he was able to give a performance of *Faust* at the

Conservatoire on 15 April. In 1850 he became president and chief conductor of the Société Philharmonique. It was at his own suggestion and he had in mind the London Philharmonic Society as his model. It lasted only until March 1851. He made a second visit to London, and was French representative at the Great Exhibition (with the Crystal Palace in Hyde Park) in May for makers of musical instruments. He was confident that France led in this field by virtue of the work of Érard, Sax* and Wuillaume (the old sore caused him to ignore the contribution of Pleyel to the evolution of musical instrument design and construction). He stayed at 27 Queen Anne Street, Cavendish Square.† His *Te Deum* had been finished for two years and was still unperformed. Could London offer him the opportunity for it?

His wanderings in London led him to St Paul's Cathedral, where he was tremendously impressed by the singing of the Charity School children. Before returning to Paris he accepted the post of conductor of the newly formed New Philharmonic Society orchestra and in March 1852 made a third visit to London to conduct its first concert. Because of this engagement he had to miss Liszt's production of *Benvenuto Cellini* at Weimar on 20 March. He conducted six concerts during the spring and early summer of 1852, including two memorable performances of Beethoven's Ninth symphony. He had arrived with Marie Recio on 24 March and stayed this time at 10 Cavendish Street.

Some dead affairs rise up to haunt former lovers. At Exeter Hall on 28 April 1852 the third of the New Philharmonic Society concerts had Berlioz as conductor and Marie Felicité Denise (Camille) Pleyel as soloist in Weber's *Concertstück*. In 1830 Berlioz, passionately in love with Camille Moke (as she then was), had written to his sister Nanci, 'She is nearly as tall as me, figure slim and graceful, with magnificent black hair and large blue eyes which shine like stars . . . she is lively . . . with a fundamentally kind nature . . . at the piano she is Corinna—her talent has something miraculous about it.' Then she betrayed Berlioz, and the vision and adoration turned sour; even his judgement of her talent went by the board. By 1845 he judged her playing as 'elegant but shallow and attempting to simulate feeling by affected changes of time'. When Berlioz wrote those somewhat severe words, many considered Camille Pleyel the peer of Liszt! Otherwise his critical judgement was sound, and it is unlikely that personal prejudice, that most unprofessional intrusion into critical judgement,

*Adolphe Sax was in fact a Belgian. He too was in London for the 1851 Exhibition. Berlioz wrote: 'Skilful composers will hereafter get admirable effects from the saxophone, in combinations which would be rash to try to foresee.'

†Byron had been born, on 22 January 1788, at 16 Holles Street. Holles Street was a lane which ran between Oxford Street and Cavendish Square. All traces vanished in the Blitz of 1940, but the street name is preserved. The site is near 27 Queen Anne Street, where Berlioz stayed in 1851.

really affected Berlioz. There was, indeed, something shallow about Camille: her husband cast her aside within five years of marriage, for infidelity and wild behaviour. She also smoked the strongest cigars, and was notorious for a large number of tempestuous love affairs.

After the April concert Camille, more or less predictably, complained that the conducting had ruined her playing. Berlioz in turn complained about her performance. So at subsequent concerts Dr Henry Wylde conducted whenever Camille played, and a Mlle Clause played the piano when Berlioz conducted. Thus the former lovers were discreetly kept apart and musical harmony prevailed.

Berlioz's return to Paris in June 1852 was ignored by the French musical élite. He visited Weimar in November for two successful performances of *Benvenuto Cellini*. This encouraged him to present the opera in London during his 1853 visit, when it was produced at Covent Garden on 25 June. It was a total failure. The Italian artists in London were particularly anti-Berlioz, perpetuating Franco-Italian musical animosities; his English friends though attempted (but failed) to organize a benefit concert for him at Exeter Hall.

His 1853 return to Paris was again barren, so he took the opportunity to pay another visit to Germany, to give concerts at Baden-Baden, Frankfurt, Hanover, Bremen and Leipzig, where he heard the youthful Brahms, then aged twenty, play at a private reception. Berlioz was most favourably impressed.

1854 was a depressing year for Berlioz. Harriet died, it was his duty to marry Marie Recio, he travelled in Europe, his friends Liszt and von Bülow failed to obtain for him Wagner's former post of conductor at the Dresden Royal Opera. On 1 April he wrote to Roquemont, from Hanover, on a happier note:

... on learning of my arrival, the King of Hanover gave orders for the artistes, singers and others who were to appear in the last concert given by the Société Philharmonique to be countermanded; he wished the programme to be changed to include nothing but music by me. The Queen sent to ask me to put in at least two pieces from *Roméo*, the Adagio and Queen Mab.

In 1855 he was still travelling. February found him at Gotha and Weimar, where a Berlioz week was given and Joachim Raff composed a Latin cantata in his honour, he conducted the first performance of Liszt's E flat piano concerto, and the Princess Sayn-Wittgenstein suggested to him that he should write an opera on the subject of the Trojans based on Virgil's *Aeneid*. He returned to Paris in May 1855, but as usual there was no great welcome, so the following month he made yet another visit to London.

He had fond memories of London. Part I of his 'Dramatic Symphony' *Roméo et Juliette* had been well received at Exeter Hall. This majestic building was entered through a narrow frontage on the

Strand which consisted of a tall portico formed by two handsome Corinthian pillars, with steps from street level to the door of the hall. Berlioz wrote to Liszt on 24 March: '. . . I have just had a most glorious success at Exeter Hall, and that at the very time when you were conducting the second performance of *Benvenuto* at Weimar'; and the *Literary Gazette* had reported, 'the Hall was filled, 1500, all in evening dress'. The expected euphoria did not, however, come to him on a salver. As ever, there was conflict and contention as well as success. On 3 July he wrote to the Parisian composer—pianist Théodore Ritter, 'Yesterday a frightful rehearsal at Exeter Hall, Glover's* cantata, in a piquant style, but difficult, which made me sweat enough to swell the gutters in the Strand, and the Finale of *Harold* and a ferocious concerto by Henselt played by Klindworth[†] in a free style, which kept me dancing on the slack rope for an hour . . .' To add to the confusion, the trumpet players were delayed because of the rehearsal of Meyerbeer's opera *Etoile du Nord* at Covent Garden.

By 1855 the influence of Berlioz was at its height, thanks to the appreciation shown by countries other than his own. Nevertheless, the French school of symphonic music was directly affected by his compositions through the work of Saint-Saëns, Gounod, Bizet, Massenet and others who admired him and gave the lead to the younger French ideal. And he was reaping some reward. The seeming chaos of London rehearsals led to 'success on the night' in a typically English tradition of public performance. From his London lodgings at 13 Margaret Street he wrote on 23 June to François Rety, the cashier (later auditor) at the Paris Conservatoire—'My affairs are going splendidly, better, in fact, than ever before.'

Novello, the publishers, were interested in Berlioz's *Treatise on Instrumentation*, written in 1844 and already becoming a standard text book, and wanted to bring out an English translation. He replied—

69 Dean Street, Soho, June 30, 1855, to Alfred Novello, London Music Publisher,
Dear Sir,

I have the letter in which you invite me to revise my *Treatise on Instrumentation* for an English edition, and to enlarge it by adding a few chapters, this to be done for the sum of forty pounds, payable on delivery of the manuscript this September. I accept your offer and its terms,
    Yours very truly,
    Hector Berlioz.

---

*Probably Stephen Glover (1812–70), a worthily prolific composer of the period.
[†]Professor Karl Klindworth, born in Hanover in 1830 and died in 1916 at Oranienburg, Berlin, which became a notorious concentration camp under the Nazis during World War II. In 1852 a Jewish woman advanced him money to study with Liszt. He made his music début in London in 1854 and became a friend of Wagner. Between 1854 and 1868 he gave concerts and lessons in London.

And from his Paris address, 19 rue Boursault, on 13 September he again wrote to Alfred Novello,

. . . sends the corrections and manuscript of *Treatise on Instrumentation* plus the *Theory of the Conductor's Art* . . . it is difficult to translate such things into another language in a way that is *clear*.

    With best regards,
      Hector Berlioz.

Berlioz was greeted with proper regard on his second trip to Paris in 1855: Napoleon III conferred a gold medal on him in November. The *Te Deum* had been performed, his *Treatise on Instrumentation* had been revised and augmented, his song cycle *Les Nuits d'été* had been revised and orchestrated, and the chaos of his life as a composer had been 'tidied up'. He owed much to the recognition and encouragement he had received in London and during his other travels in Europe. He was now ready for the final phase of his life. He would slow down the pace of his trips abroad. They had served their purpose; they had established him. He could at last relax a little from the constant fight for fair play against intrigue and petty bickering. He could concentrate on a new and mighty work, the lyric drama *Les Troyens*. He could now compose, revise, put his work in order, so that historians and lovers of his music could follow development from the time of his discovery that he was to be a composer to the achievement of his greatest works.

THE BALLET OF THE SHADES

MIDNIGHT REVEL

for Chorus and Piano
Words by Albert Duboys, after Herder
Music by
HECTOR BERLIOZ
Edited, with English words, by Hugh Macdonald

'Tis now the very witching time of night
When churchyards yawn, and hell itself breathes out
Contagion to this world...

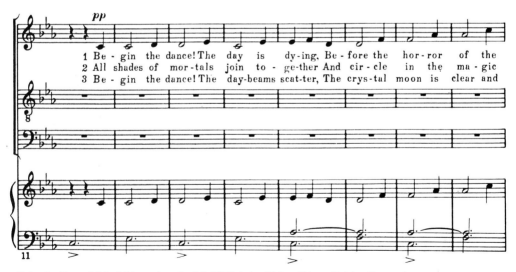

Note: Berlioz published this work as Op.2 in 1829, but withdrew it immediately afterwards.
The first tenors sing with the sopranos an octave lower throughout. Altos may join either the sopranos or the second tenors.

19778

MADE IN ENGLAND

The luxurious interior of the
Opéra-Comique.

7 The Final Years

The last thirteen years of Berlioz's life, spent at his twelfth Paris address (17 rue Vintimille, later 4 rue de Calais), had more than their fair share of sadness, brightened perhaps by a reluctant admission by the French that he was after all a major composer. There were also the occasional—and with Berlioz inevitable—escapades into the bewildering ecstasies and entanglements of love. During the 1859 revival of Gluck's *Orphée* he fell in love with Pauline Viardot, wife of the impresario Louis Viardot and inamorata of the Russian novelist and short-story master Ivan Turgenev. Like Marie Recio, Pauline had Spanish connections, in fact was born in Spain. She was also a mezzo soprano.

It was during these last years in Paris that Berlioz's two late masterpieces for the musical theatre came into being. He had always been attracted to the theatre indeed, his particular genius was essentially theatrical, but he had no great opinion of the current operatic practices. He had long wooed the operatic theatre, diligently but without success, notably with *Benvenuto Cellini*. Whether because of this or because of the natural evolution of his genius he had subsequently been exploring a new kind of dramatic music, in *La Damnation de Faust*, *Roméo et Juliette* and, latterly, *L'Enfance du Christ*. The question of whether these belong to the theatre or the concert hall will probably never be fully answered. He himself described his *Faust* as '*opéra de concert*', *Roméo et Juliette* as '*symphonie dramatique*', and *L'Enfance du Christ* as a '*trilogie sacrée*'. But such descriptions do not in themselves mean very much.

The failure of *Benvenuto Cellini* had several causes. It seems to have been doomed to fiasco from the start. Partly it was due to the inept handling of the subject by his librettists, Barbier and de Wailly, who made virtually nothing of Cellini's colourful autobiography. Yet some of the material was handled with great brilliance by Berlioz, like the famous 'Roman Carnival' scene, dramatically unique against the somewhat rigid convention of the Parisian opera of the day. The most serious cause of the failure was inadequate performance. Berlioz wrote:

I shall never forget the horror of those three months (May–August 1838). The indifference, the distaste manifested by most of the singers (who were already convinced that it would be a flop); Haberneck's ill humour, and the vague rumours that were constantly going round the theatre . . . but which I had pretended not to notice.

Pauline Viardot, the mezzo soprano with whom Berlioz fell in love in 1859.

Haberneck infuriated Berlioz by taking the Salterello so slowly that the dancers were put off. A few years later (1844) Berlioz himself conducted this Salterello, which he used as a theme in his *Le Carnaval romain*. He took it *allegro*, and then, as he passed Haberneck in the wings, hissed: 'That's how it goes!' Cartoonists, mocking the opera, changed the name from 'Benvenuto' (the welcome one) to 'Malvenuto' (the unwelcome one). The Opéra-Comique at first declined the Barbier/Wailly libretto, and this should have alerted Berlioz to the unpopularity of his chosen theme. It probably would have remained so even if it had been better handled, for there were non-musical and non-dramatic elements in the situation. Benvenuto Cellini was a sixteenth century Florentine sculptor and goldsmith who advocated the artist as hero, a philosophy adopted by the French Romantics (indeed, by the Romantic movement in general). Opera in France was Italian dominated, and despite the subject of Berlioz's opera the Italians cosily established in Paris were not keen to support a possible school of French romantic opera—hence the Italian opposition in both Paris and London.

There was nevertheless money and fame in opera, and on his return from Italy Berlioz, influenced by the fame and wealth of Meyerbeer following the success of *Robert le diable*, decided that his best way to obtain recognition was through opera. The same year, 1833, he requested the loan of Shakespeare's *Much Ado About Nothing* from Joseph-Louis d'Ortigue and contemplated writing a lively opera based on it. What a pity he didn't! *Béatrice et Bénédict* written in 1833 instead of thirty years later might have brought him the success he was seeking. He was married to a famous Shakespearean actress, his son Louis was born (August 1834), and his little two-act caprice, which did not succeed in the 1860s, might well have been a hit in the 1830s. Indeed, it might have set the fashion for the 'Folies de Paris' of the second half of the nineteenth century and been the French equivalent of the Gilbert and Sullivan comic operettas in England. 'Recognition' certainly, but surely not the sort he was after. He must have realized that his unique strength lay in orchestral writing, whether or not combined with voices.

It was not until near the end of his life that Berlioz made his second attempt to write opera, serious or otherwise. He began work on *Les Troyens* in 1856. The Princess Sayn-Wittgenstein had suggested the idea in 1855, after revealing to Berlioz Wagner's great plan for *The Ring*; he sent her the text in July 1856 and completed the work in April 1858. But the score lay around for five years, and Berlioz despaired of ever seeing it performed. It had taken Berlioz back to his early love of Virgil. It came out as a huge musico-dramatic edifice, so much so that he decided he must be practical and divide it into two parts—*La Prise de Troie* (three acts) and *Les Troyens à Carthage* (four acts), thus producing two separate though linked

Opera composers in Berlioz's day achieved money, fame—and honour of a sort, adorning the ornate walls of the Paris Opéra.

entities. The complete work (both parts) was not given until 1890, and then in a German version at Carlsruhe; but *Les Troyens à Carthage* was produced in Paris, at the Théâtre-Lyrique in November 1863. After a second performance Berlioz wrote to his friend Richard Pohl, 'the 2nd performance of *Les Troyens* was given yesterday and far surpassed even the brilliance of the first; it aroused feelings I shall not attempt to describe. Mme Charton is superb as Dido; you would not believe her capable of such lofty tragedy.'

It is not unreasonable to see *Les Troyens* (complete) and *The Ring of the Nibelungen* as the two great complementary and characteristic musico-dramatic productions of the age of Romanticism in the nineteenth century. Musical history tends to see the 'split' after the death of Beethoven as going one way with Wagner, the other with Brahms. As far as the Central European tradition, based on Germany, is concerned, that is true. But there was at least one other way for music to go, and that is the way Berlioz took, with *Les Troyens*. Berlioz wished to bring back to opera, albeit in a new and revitalized form, the set numbers and formal designs that Wagner was decisively rejecting. The music of Berlioz presents that apparently paradoxical but in fact very French combination of classical style and proportion and romantic sensibility. And there is also his great debt to Gluck, that master of 'reformed' opera: Berlioz believed that it was Gluck and not Wagner who pointed the true way forward for musical drama. Yet if Wagner disliked and distrusted Berlioz's great work, he was not deceived about Berlioz's stature and quality. When Berlioz died, Wagner said that 'some day a grateful France will raise a proud monument on his tomb'. It took a long time, but it came about.

Berlioz's tombstone in Montmartre Cemetery.

Difficulties over finding the right singers for Berlioz's music affected his late works too, including *Les Troyens*. He maintained that the only singer capable of performing Dido was Anne Arsène Charton-Demeur. She created the rôles of Béatrice in 1862 and Dido in 1863, and ten years after Berlioz's death, when she herself was fifty-four, she sang Cassandra in the first concert performances of Acts I and II of *Les Troyens à Carthage*. Berlioz said that Anne Arsène sang with warmth, delicacy, great energy, and rare beauty of style. After Marie Recio died, Anne Arsène became a very close friend of Berlioz and was at his bedside when he himself died. Towards the end of the nineteenth century Marie Cornélie Falcon was considered to be one of the best exponents of Berlioz. She had sung the lead in Louise Bertin's opera *Esmeralda* in 1836, and had taken part in a Berlioz concert at the Conservatoire as far back as 1834. Pauline Viadot, sister of Maria Malibran and daughter of Manuel Garcia the great singing teacher, sang Cassandra in *Les Troyens à Carthage* in Baden in 1859. Berlioz fell in love with her after they had both worked on the 1859 revival of *Orphée*. Pauline sang the duet from *Béatrice et Bénédict* with Madame Vandenteuvel-Duprez, Berlioz enthusing that the pair sang it exquisitely: 'It was one of those performances one sometimes hears in dreams.' In the *Musical Quarterly*, 1915, Vol. I, Pauline recalled a long walk she took with Berlioz, and he said to her, 'My whole life has been one of ardent pursuit of an ideal formed in my own imagination. Whenever I found a single quality belonging to that ideal, my heart, eager for love, seized on it . . .' Rosina Stoltz, as we have seen, was much put out when she did not get the part of Dido.

Covent Garden produced *Les Troyens* complete in 1957 and 1969. Josephine Veasey gave a stupendous rendering of Dido, using the full range of her voice, and portraying the passions of tenderness or despair with queenly dignity. These performances would have delighted Berlioz, as would the 1972 Last Night of the Proms, with hundreds of young people singing, 'Hail, All Hail to the Queen!' from *Les Troyens*, which might well have brought back his own days in London and Jullien's popular concerts.*

The death of Dido should have been his own glorious swan-song, but a new opera was required for Baden-Baden, hence the (belated?) writing of *Béatrice et Bénédict*. This vivacious *opéra-comique* was performed on 9 August 1862, and a tired old Berlioz vowed he would write no more.

On the personal plane, Berlioz's last years were not happy. Marie died of a heart attack on 13 June 1862. It had not been a love match and there had been differences, especially over her determination to

*A concert performance of *Les Troyens* was used to open the 1982 season of Henry Wood Promenade concerts in London.

sing. But she had been his companion for more than twenty years and his second wife for many of them. In 1865 Berlioz sent the finished text of his *Memoirs* to the printers, to be ready for publication in July, at his own expense. They were to be published by his son Louis, a sea captain. In 1867 Louis died in Havana of yellow fever. It was a shattering blow. Hector and his son were very close. Louis, his only child, wrote, 'I could not love my father more than I do already . . . God alone can measure the depth of affection there is between us . . . The thread of my life is but the extension of my father's. When it is cut, both lives will end.' It turned out very much like that.

There was still something for Berlioz to do, however, before he was ready for death to claim him. He had to return to his first love, make a pilgrimage to Meylan to see Estelle once more. When they met, she said: 'We are very old acquaintances, you and I, M. Berlioz . . . We were children together.' The dying Berlioz spoke with his 'Stella montis' for some time. She had six children, of whom two were dead by the time Berlioz reappeared in 1864. The moment to go came all too quickly:

'Madam, give me your hand.'
She held it out to me at once. I carried it to my lips and felt my heart turn to water and a thrill shoot through every bone in my body.
'May I hope,' I said, after another silence, 'that you will allow me to write to you sometimes, and very occasionally visit you?'
'Oh yes, indeed. But I shall not be in Lyons much longer . . . Goodbye, M. Berlioz: I am deeply grateful for the feelings that you still have for me.'
I bowed and took her hand again, held it for a moment to my forehead, and had the strength to go.

A regular and on his part ardent correspondence ensued between them. It was to Estelle he turned for solace at the time of his son's death.

29.6.1867. 4 rue de Calais. To Estelle Fornier.
Forgive me for turning to you in a time when I am stricken by the greatest loss I have ever experienced. My poor son died in Havana, aged thirty-three.

The walk from the twelfth Paris address of Berlioz to his final resting place is extremely short. A hundred yards west of 4 rue de Calais one comes to a square, now known as Square Berlioz. It is iron-fenced, well planted with trees and shrubs, and inside is an oval area with seats. These face a rectangular sandpit where children can play. Overlooking this scene is a statue of Berlioz. A few yards southwards down rue Vintimille is a crossroads known as Place Lili-Boulanger, in memory of the first woman to win the Prix de Rome. Northwards from Square Berlioz is a narrow lane, rue P. Haret, only about forty yards long, which leads into the wide Boulevard de Clichy. On the other side of the Boulevard, the most congested

116

thoroughfare in Paris at night-time, is the quiet, unnoticed Avenue Rachel, which leads to the south-eastern gate of the Montmartre cemetery, no more than fifty yards from the busy pleasure-bent boulevard. At the gate entrance there is a bell, and as each funeral stops at the gate the bell is rung, even today, and then the procession enters. At the north-east corner of the cemetery, running in a westerly direction, is Avenue Hector Berlioz, and about thirty yards from the corner is Berlioz's grave.

When Marie died in 1862 she was buried in one of the small cemeteries in Montmartre. A good friend of Berlioz, Edouard Alexandre, who became one of his executors, bought a plot of land in

The statue of Berlioz that dominates the square bearing his name.

117

the large Montmartre cemetery. Berlioz had to witness Marie's exhumation and reinterment in the new grave. This deeply affected him. Shortly afterwards he was informed that the small grave where Harriet lay was in a cemetery due to be abolished, and did he want the remains? On 23 February 1864 Berlioz had to witness a grave-digger jump into the opened grave, pull away the rotting planks instead of lifting out the coffin, and with his bare hands drop the bones and skull of 'fair Ophelia' into a new coffin. This was then taken to the main cemetery of Montmartre, Berlioz grimly following the hearse down the hill. The two dead women lay in the same grave, awaiting the time when, to quote Berlioz, 'I shall bring my own share of corruption to the same charnel-house.'

The 'charnel-house' is now a beautiful black marble gravestone, erected by public subscription on the initiative of Henri Poussigue in 1970, to celebrate the centenary of the composer's death. The circular picture on the large headstone is a bronze reproduction of the drawing by Cyp Godebjk made in 1889, and the disc was cast by Husset, Foundeur, Paris.

In the *Memoirs* David Cairns, editor of the 1969 Victor Gollancz edition, briefly describes the end:

He took to his bed in January, and sank gradually into a coma. Friends visited him—the Damckes, Saint-Saëns, Reyer; and he would half rise to greet them; but he was silent, and could only smile. His mother-in-law and Madame Charton-Demeur, his first Dido, were with him when he died, at 12.30 p.m. on 8th March 1869.

Bibliography

Hector Berlioz, *Memoirs* (ed. & trans. David Cairns), Victor Gollancz, London 1969.

Hector Berlioz, *Evenings with the Orchestra* (trans. C. R. Fortescue), Penguin Books, Harmondsworth 1963; also (trans. J. Barzun) Alfred Knopf, New York 1956.

Hector Berlioz, *Treatise on Instrumentation*, Novello, London 1904.

Hector Berlioz, 'Beethoven's Nine Symphonies' and 'Mozart, Weber and Wagner', in *A Travers Chants* (trans. Edwin Evans), William Reeves, London 1969.

Michael Ayrton, *Berlioz: A Singular Obsession*, BBC Publications, London 1969.

Henry Barraud *et al*, *Hector Berlioz: Génies et Réalitiés*, Réalitiés-Hachette, Paris 1973.

J. Barzun, *New Letters*, Columbia University Press, New York 1954.

P. E. Charvet (trans.), *Baudelaire: Selected Writings on Art and Artists*, Cambridge University Press, Cambridge 1981.

John Crabbe, *Hector Berlioz: Rational Romantic*, Stanmore Press, London 1980.

J. H. Elliott, *Berlioz*. J. M. Dent & Sons, London 1982.

Hans Gal, *Letters of the Great Composers*, Thames & Hudson, London 1965.

A. W. Ganz, *Berlioz in London*, Quality Press, London 1950.

Cecil Hopkinson, *Bibliography of the Musical and Literary Works of Hector Berlioz*, printed for the Edinburgh Bibliographical Society, Edinburgh 1951.

Robert Hughes (comp.), *Music Lovers' Encyclopedia*, Universal Textbooks Ltd, London (undated).

Alan Kendall, *Music: Its Story in the West*, W. H. Smith, London 1980.

Francoise Lesure, *Debussy, On Music*, Secker & Warburg, London 1977.

Edward Lockspeiser, *Berlioz*, Novello, London (undated).

Hugh MacDonald, *Berlioz's Orchestral Music*, BBC Music Guides, London 1969.

H. Mainwaring Dunstan (trans.), *Life and Letters of Berlioz*, Remington & Co., London.

Derek Parker, *Byron, His World*, Thames & Hudson, London 1968.

Stanley Sadie (ed.), *The New Grove's Dictionary of Music and Musicians*, Macmillan & Co., London 1954.

Percy M. Scholes, *Oxford Companion to Music* (7th ed.), Oxford University Press, Oxford 1947.

Robert Simpson (ed.), *The Symphony: Haydn to Dvořák*, Penguin Books, Harmondsworth 1966.

D. F. Tovey, *Essays in Musical Analysis*, vol. IV, Oxford University Press, Oxford 1946.

W. J. Turner, *Berlioz (Book IV, 1843–69)*, J. M. Dent & Sons, London 1934.

Index

Selective list of references
Illustrations are indicated in bold type

122

DATE